# CANBERRA

## IN THE WAKE OF A LEGEND

To Jürgen Reschmeke
With best wishes from your
brother-in-law

Toronto, 10 May 1997

# CANBERRA

## IN THE WAKE OF A LEGEND

### PHILIP DAWSON

Conway Maritime Press
in conjunction with
P&O Cruises

# AUTHOR'S ACKNOWLEDGMENTS

It is for me a great privilege and honour to write this tribute to *Canberra*. However, a project such as this is never the work of one person, but rather a collaborative effort of many people who conspire in various ways to bring it all together. It has been a great pleasure to work with Nicki Marshall as project manager at Conway, whose quick grasp of the essence of *Canberra*, and whose determination and hard work in collating pictures and chasing permissions have been key to bringing the book together. My thanks also to John Lee for his managerial, business and technical assistance, and to David McLean for his personal hospitality during my research visit to London last year.

The support of P&O has been absolutely first-rate, right from the kindness of Lord Sterling in writing the Foreword to the efforts of many P&O Group and P&O Cruises staff who have helped in so many ways. I am particularly grateful to Kay Davidson, who did much of the legwork to get this project underway from P&O's standpoint. Nick Burnett, Len Stuckey, David Dingle, Lyn Palmer, Melissa Brain and Sue Cox were all kind enough to take time out of their busy schedules to meet with Nicki and myself, to answer our questions, gather information and make arrangements for us to meet other personnel. My thanks, once again, to P&O's information manager, Stephen Rabson, who has been a veritable 'guardian angel' to me over the years and who so generously gave us the benefit of his own great knowledge and P&O's vast archives. Thanks also to Stephen Payne for his invaluable comments.

*Canberra*'s own remarkable hospitality was shown, as ever, through the good graces of her master, Captain Rory Smith, who convened his long-serving hands for a fascinating discussion in his day room during the ship's last refit, and who made his ship available to me. I am particularly grateful to Christopher Rodriguez for his perspective of the crew life, and for taking me behind the scenes to where few passengers have had the privilege of going.

When I first sailed aboard *Canberra* in 1982 Captain Mike Bradford opened many doors to me aboard his ship and at P&O, which gave me a profound understanding of *Canberra*'s workings. Last November I had the great pleasure of Commodore and Mrs Bradford's hospitality at their home, with former captain Jock Lefevre also joining us for the day. I also had the very special privilege of visiting Commodore Ian Gibb and his family at home, as well as talking with Peter Wise and Jim Davis, whose insight into the management side of things was most valuable.

Unfortunately, the very tight time scale of the project did not allow for more such meetings, as there were many others who would have loved to share their memories of *Canberra*. Alice Lovely's kindness of a telephone interview and a delightful correspondence with Margaret Mchugh in Australia have been indispensable in allowing me to see the ship more broadly through the eyes of other passengers to whom the ship is so special.

There are many others who have been most helpful, not least my wife, Ingrid, who proof read the text and offered various suggestions for improvement.

To all whose names space does not permit me to mention, you are nonetheless in my thoughts and please accept my sincere thanks for helping to make this book the perfect tribute to a magnificent ship.

© Conway Maritime Press, 1997

First published in Great Britain in 1997 by Conway Maritime Press, an imprint of Brassey's (UK) Ltd, 33 John Street, London WC1N 2AT

ISBN 0-85177-707-4

**British Library Cataloguing in Publication Data**
Dawson, Philip S.
    Canberra : in the wake of a legend
    1. Canberra (Ship) - History
    I. Title II. P&O Cruises
    387.2'432'09

Designed by Peter Champion

Printed and bound by The University Press, Cambridge

# CONTENTS

QUIS NOS SEPARABIT

# FOREWORD

The retirement of a ship is always reason for a moment of reflection and never more so than when the ship concerned is a great ocean liner such as *Canberra*. This proud ship has served P&O impeccably over a long and illustrious career; she has won many friends and admirers among those who have sailed aboard her whether as passengers or as crew, and she touched the hearts of millions with her valiant service in the Falklands Campaign.

No ship can go on forever and it was with great sadness that the decision was taken to retire *Canberra* in September 1997. By allowing her to go gracefully, whilst still delivering all that her passengers expect and hope for, we will ensure that her reputation remains untarnished.

The world has changed a great deal since *Canberra* was first launched in 1961; indeed, within a few years of the ship's introduction, the role for which she was built - that of liner voyages to Australia - had virtually disappeared and it seemed as though *Canberra* would have to be scrapped.

However, her successful transition to cruise ship ensured her survival for the next twenty-five years. From emigrants looking forward to a new life in Australia, to world travellers and families basking in the sun for two weeks, *Canberra* has faithfully served nearly a million passengers.

This book is for all those who have enjoyed crossing the seas aboard this great ship, who have worked on the ship or in any way been associated with her, and it is for those who have perhaps seen her from afar and wondered what the 'Great White Whale' was really like. This is not just a 'goodbye' but also a 'thank you' to a ship, the like of which will not be seen again.

*St ⌐ ⌐ Plaistow*

The Lord Sterling of Plaistow, CBE
Chairman, The Peninsular and
Oriental Steam Navigation Company

*The coat of arms of the Peninsular and Oriental Steam Navigiation Company.*

# INTRODUCTION
# BERTH OF A LEGEND

When the P&O Line started to promote their largest-ever new passenger ship to the travelling public in the 1950s, they coined the phrase 'The ship which shapes the future'. The sentiment this expressed actually ran much deeper than the ocean-going modern living it promised for the day her first passengers would board for the maiden voyage to Sydney and Auckland. This new ship's future would itself see unprecedented change which would at the same time reshape the very basis of her existence, along with that of her owners, the countries and peoples she would serve, and see vast increases in competition from the air and in public fortune and mobility.

This new ship would ultimately have to survive and flourish in one of the most illustrious periods

Canberra *during her later career as a cruise ship passing through the Gaillard Cut in the Panama Canal.*

P&O has a long history of passages to the Orient; 'passing the homeward-bound Victoria in the Suez Canal', from William Whitelock Lloyd's P&O Pencillings, published in 1890.

in the history of modern civilisation. She would emerge into the jet age and into an era of international modernity, progress and liberalisation. This was an optimistic period of growth which appeared to have the momentum to go on for ever. It produced phenomenal increases in personal wealth and freedom; the 'masses' attained mobility and greater amounts of free time to travel and enjoy themselves. The private automobile came into its own within the financial reach of the average household, overseas travel became more attainable and more people than ever before were able to buy their own homes. There was a far more liberal expression of ideas and images in the arts and letters. Glossy magazines and the emerging medium of television chronicled these developments throughout the world, while they also were glamourised in films and novels.

However, the optimism and self-assuredness of the times were to some degree born out of the need of a badly war-damaged world to rebuild and repair vast devastation both materially and emotionally. It had also to realign itself to new political boundaries and orders and to repatriate and relocate many of its peoples. On the darker side, these were also the days of the Cold War, the partitioning of India and the Suez Crisis.

By the late 1940s, the traditional passenger trades to the Far East and to Australia, which had been pioneered and developed by P&O and the Orient Line, were changing irrevocably. The partitioning of India into the separate Dominions of India and Pakistan in 1947, and the independence of Ceylon and Burma in 1948, were significantly to effect the trading patterns of both lines. Their long-established roles in providing necessary services for government officials, troops and mails moving to and from the motherland, were finally and irreversibly curtailed. While essential services farther afield to the Far East and Oceania remained intact, along with a consistent diet of 'assisted passages' for those emigrating to Australia, the trading positions of these lines was further jeopardised by new and unfamiliar competition.

This came not only from the stratosphere and the opening of new long-haul international air

routes, but also from new rivals at sea level. The immediate post-Second World War era, with its vast exodus of British and other European peoples effectively 'displaced' from their war-ravaged homelands, had produced a seemingly insatiable demand for liner services to all parts of the globe. Lauro Lines, Sitmar (absorbed into the P&O group's Princess Cruises in 1988) and Chandris emerged from the Mediterranean to compete head-to-head with long-established lines such as P&O, Orient (which P&O had controlled since 1918) and Lloyd Triestino.

At the same time, alternative opportunities were being studied. Australia was no longer looking primarily to Britain for trade, but rather to new opportunities across the Pacific Ocean to the north and east. Her commercial links with Japan, the United States, Canada, Malaya, China and New Zealand were opening up the potential for Pacific rim services to and from Sydney. New triangular routes linking Australia with the Far East and the North American west coast were started in 1954

forming an amalgamated P&O/Orient Australian-Pacific Far Eastern passenger and cargo services network. The joining of Orient Line's original Australian route with the traditional Far Eastern services of P&O, along with the extensions of new Pacific routes to Britain and Europe eastward via the Panama Canal, gave the combined services a complete round-the-world capability of the sort being offered by Shaw Savill's then brand new *Southern Cross*. The position of P&O and Orient Line in the Pacific was further strengthened by the 1953 terminations of Canadian Australasian Line's transpacific services to Vancouver and of Matson's passenger services to the United States.

Integrated Pacific services, which were operated under the name Orient & Pacific Lines, provided an extensive network of routes. These included a Sydney to North America service with stops at Suva and Honolulu, a Far East service from Sydney to Manila, Hong Kong and Yokohama or Kobe and an alternative transpacific Australia to United Kingdom service, via Los Angeles, the

*A*rab youngsters following a P&O ship for 'baksheesh' or gratuities, and mooring and undocking using semaphore signals to communicate with the bridge during the 1890s, as depicted by William Whitelock Lloyd.

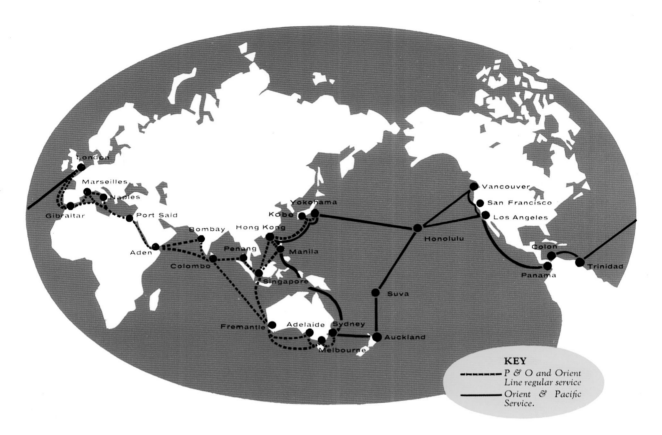

*The network of Pacific Ocean and round-the-world
services for which the new superliners* Oriana *and*
Canberra *would be built.*

Panama Canal and Le Havre. There was also a connection between the Far East and North American routes providing the option of sailing from Yokohama to Honolulu, forming a triangle with the North American West Coast ports of Los Angeles, San Francisco and Vancouver. This made a special Pacific Circle ticket possible for holiday travellers. While American President Lines' own plans for their 43,000-ton 29-knot ship, *President Washington*, seemed to be getting bogged down in the late 1950s, these developments were seen in the United States as a strong British bid for supremacy on the Pacific.

The Pacific was also viewed as a vast untapped reservoir of opportunity. With faster ships designed exclusively for passenger service, where time in port could be reduced without the need to handle cargo, it would be possible to add Pacific destinations to the regular liner voyages to and from Britain. This offered great possibilities as the then P&O deputy chairman Sir Donald Anderson explained:

We are breaking new ground, though we have to do a good deal more breaking yet. With passengers, emigrants from the United Kingdom to Australia and bringing back businessmen, students and tourists; we are taking businessmen and tourists from Australia to America; and we are taking tourists from North America to the Far East, and in increasing numbers direct from the Pacific coast to Europe.

From the standpoint of tourism and leisure travel, the cultural diversity of those nations surrounding the Pacific and the immense natural beauty of such celebrated tropical paradises as Hawaii and Fiji had much to offer. Itineraries which would together serve the line traffic and leisure trade were to continue being developed, not only in the vast localised area of the Pacific but also in the British market, where increasing numbers of people had the time and money to book holiday voyages out of Southampton.

By the mid 1950s P&O and Orient Lines both realised that the type of ships needed for so great a diversity of services over such long distances would have to be considerably faster, and thus substantially larger than the latest 22.5-knot 28,000-ton liners then in their service. The most logical increment in speed was to 27.5 knots, which would fit in with their long and complex routings more than half way around the globe, reducing the round voyage time from England to Australia and New Zealand by a full two weeks. This allowed a reduction of one full day each in the voyage's long Southampton - Port Said, Suez - Colombo and Colombo - Fremantle sea segments, both outward and home-bound. Time was also to be saved through careful planning and scheduling of the many port calls along the way.

Arrivals were organised for early mornings so that stevedoring and other commercial operations could be completed in a single shift, with the ship ready to sail late afternoon or early evening on the same day. Planned early arrivals at Aden and Port Said would allow the ship to immediately join a convoy for passage through the Suez Canal in either direction without losing valuable time. Outbound, ten hours had to be allowed at Aden for bunkering. Homeward-bound, a stop at Naples was substituted for the outward call at Marseilles, avoiding a costly evening arrival in the French

*Sir Donald Anderson, then P&O's deputy chairman, whose vision of the future so influenced the building of* Oriana *and* Canberra.

port, with stevedoring and passenger disembarking formalities only starting the following morning.

Still more time could theoretically have been saved by doing away with all but the operationally-essential port calls. From the human standpoint of passengers and crew alike these calls are necessary to alleviate fatigue, monotony and stress resulting from long uninterrupted periods at sea – anything more that five or so days at a stretch has long been considered too many, especially for cruise passengers where the voyage itself is the holiday. In the extended portion of the voyages across the Pacific,

sightseeing would be an important consideration in planning the itineraries. Long-haul non-stop services would ultimately become the speciality of the airlines, where jetlag is accepted as a minor side effect of swift passage. As well laid as the route's planning was, it also had to allow for intervention by the powerful hand of Nature. Atlantic storms in the Bay of Biscay, the mistrals off the south of France and seasonal monsoons in the Indian Ocean

all had to be taken into account, with the schedule allowing for time lost due to any or all of them in a single voyage to be made up.

The higher speed would also give the proposed new tonnage the range and flexibility to undertake extensive cruises in the Pacific within a reasonably short timespan of two to three weeks. This would allow, for instance, a cruise from Sydney and Auckland to Honolulu and back to be completed

*Canberra, the gentle white ship which would reduce the fatigue of long uninterrupted stretches at sea.*

in three weeks, or a one-way voyage from the same ports to Vancouver or San Francisco, with a stop in Hawaii, in about two weeks. Research carried out on Orient Line's behalf by Vickers-Armstrong, who had already built *Orcades*, *Oronsay* and *Orsova* for them between 1948 and 1954, showed that the minimum size of ship capable of economic performance at this speed would be of about 40,000 gross registered tons.

The tremendous expense of building and operating such large and fast ships was rationalised through the long-term benefits of their increased passenger capacities and reduced voyage times. This in turn would result in fewer ships of their class being needed to take care of the specified annual passenger load and to maintain the numbers of departures each year over a projected lifespan of twenty or more years. The additional fuel costs incurred for operation of the high-powered machinery that would deliver the additional five–six knots would be offset by the reduced fleet staffing levels and other economies of scale possible with two larger ships, rather than the three 28,000-tonners of the *Oronsay* or *Iberia* class that

*The public's first impression of P&O's versatile new superliners as envisaged in the eye of the artist.*

each line would otherwise need to maintain their existing service level. These economies were increased twofold by the decision of P&O and Orient Line to operate a single joint service with one new superliner each, rather than to continue running as competitors.

Both ships were ordered independently by their respective owners, with Orient's contract for *Oriana* being placed with Vickers-Armstrong of Barrow-in-Furness, while P&O's business was taken up with Harland & Wolff at Queen's Island, Belfast. The two companies had agreed to operate new ships of the same size, capacity and overall performance, but the detailed planning, structural design, engineering, interior architecture and outfitting of each ship was executed quite independently of the other. The research figures given by Vickers-Armstrong were closely followed with *Oriana*, as completed by the yard three years later. However, those of *Canberra* varied somewhat as a consequence of the radically different approach taken by her designers and builders.

The planning of such large, fast and flexible ships for the world's longest line service resulted in some rethinking of the whole concept of the traditional tropical liner. The higher speed, and the added height of the larger ships that would achieve it, called for the planning of open decks which would be protected from the high-velocity airflows created by the ship's motion and influenced by prevailing winds. With the help of extensive wind-tunnel testing, this was handled largely with full-height glass windscreens along the uppermost decks and refinements in the form of some parts of the superstructure. In *Oriana*'s case the main promenade, located high above the waterline, was fully glass enclosed, like those of her immediate North Atlantic contemporaries such as *Rotterdam* and *Leonardo da Vinci*.

Since cruising was envisioned as an important secondary role, easy amalgamation of first and tourist classes had to be taken into account. It also became necessary to provide a much higher standard of tourist class cabin accommodation than was to be found aft on the lower decks of such ships as Orient Line's relatively new *Oronsay* or P&O's *Iberia*. Accommodation in the projected ships would have to be compact enough to satisfy the need for a high capacity emigrant trade, and yet be sufficiently attractive to appeal to cruise passengers likewise occupying the rooms for periods of two or more weeks.

Italian Line's *Leonardo da Vinci*, along with Britain's *Oriana* and *Windsor Castle* were widely considered to be the three most outstanding new passenger ships of 1960. Each was specifically built for a completely different service. *Oriana*'s realm was that of the Australian trade, while *Windsor Castle* was to serve Africa, and *Leonardo da Vinci* the North Atlantic route between the Mediterranean and New York. In an article published late that year, the noted British liner critic, C M Squarey, described how modern communication and travel had narrowed the differences between various services to a single common denominator of high international standard:

> For instance suppose that the *Oriana* were put on the Southampton to New York run, the *Windsor Castle* on the Australian service and *Leonardo da Vinci* on the African route, is it likely that they would be accepted by the regular passengers on those trades as having the required amenities and in general find favour outside their normal sphere of operation?... All of them are air-conditioned so that trading in tropical waters presents no difficulties. In my view their public rooms and their cabins are perfectly acceptable for any trade.

Certainly interchangeability was beginning to be derived from the higher standards of accommodation and service being demanded on all routes. The expected cruise clientele of the 1960s would demand nothing short of air conditioning throughout the entire ship. This in itself would do away with the need for deep shade decks which had once asserted the individuality of traditional British tropical liners such as *Andes* (1939). The space could instead be used for revenue-earning cabins, bringing to the tropics something of the enclosed North Atlantic liner expression conveyed perhaps by *Rotterdam* or French Line's prestigious *France*, then building at Saint-Nazaire. Certainly the possibilities of also designing full-width public rooms, as had appeared in 1957 aboard Swedish American Lines *Gripsholm*, would warrant consideration to cater for a more diverse and sophisticated passenger lifestyle both in line service and on cruises. Indeed, fully equipped cinemas and other special rooms for various uses, along with a wider range of lounges and bars would have to be added to the obligatory main lounge, ballroom and smoking room of the P&O *Viceroy of India* (1929) and the 1930s *Straths*.

Both P&O and Orient Line had decided against the single, or hotel, class approach being tried by Shaw Savill and Union Castle. *Southern Cross* had been completed in 1955 for round-the-world service with accommodation for 1,160 passengers in an essentially all-tourist class arrangement. Later, while *Oriana* and *Canberra* were under construction, a second Shaw Savill liner of similar design was being planned, while Union Castle were likewise planning their *Transvaal Castle* to carry 728 passengers in a single class. The Union Castle ship's accommodation was arranged on the principle of a hotel, whereby all passengers would have unrestricted access to the entire suite of public rooms, passenger deck areas and other shipboard facilities. Passengers' individual needs would be met by offering a wide range of air-conditioned cabins.

*The timeless reality of Canberra's classic curvilinear form as seen underway from the air later in her career.*

*P&O chairman Sir William Currie who chose* Canberra's *name and envisaged her role in the future of Australia and the Pacific.*

*The world of* Canberra.

signed Orient Line's ship was succinctly tagged with Vickers Armstrong's yard number 1061 while her P&O opposite number was designated by Harland & Wolff as 1621. A ship's yard number remains permanently on the shipping registers, effectively as a serial number for official purposes. This and the radio call sign *Canberra* was given, GBVC, remained unchanged throughout her life. In the meantime staff at both Lines coined unofficial names of their own for the two ships, although these monikers never made it into official company circles or, heaven forbid, into the press. Following Orient's practice of starting all their liner names with the letter O, '*Orbustus*' seemed to fit well, expressing the sentiment that this fabulous

new ship was going either to make Or-bust-us. Since the all-white *Strathaird* and *Strathnaver* had set a standard of modernity of their own for P&O in the 1930s, and there had already been a *Strathmore* in 1937, the Line's largest, fastest and most expensive new liner had, in the minds of her creators, to be '*Strathmost*'.

*Oriana* was announced quite early as Orient Line's choice of name, while *Canberra*'s identity would only be disclosed on St Patrick's Day, 17 March, 1958, after construction had already started. The name is a native aborigine word meaning 'the meeting place', which had also been given to Australia's new capital city in 1913.

Another merchant ship was already registered

with the name *Canberra*, and P&O had to negotiate with its owners to make the name available to them. The vessel in question was a 2,329-ton coastal freighter owned by the Australian United Steam Navigation Company. The name *Canberra* also had a significant much earlier association with Australian passenger shipping. In 1913 the Howard Smith Company's 7,507-ton *Canberra* introduced an unprecedented standard of luxury on the route from Melbourne and Sydney to Brisbane and along the Queensland coast. She was virtually without peer for many years, with the lavishly appointed social halls and lounges for her first and second classes being of a standard, albeit on a smaller scale, normally to be found in only the most prestigious deep-sea liners of her day. This remarkable ship survived her service as a troop transport during the First World War and a disastrous fire in May 1925. Laid up after World War Two, she was sold to Greek Line in 1948, and ended up under Dominican Republic registry in 1954 before being broken up in 1969. Perhaps the fifty-six year life of this former namesake was to be a good omen for the new P&O *Canberra*'s own good fortunes.

There had also been HMAS *Canberra*, a cruiser built in 1928 for the Royal Australian Navy, which had been lost in action during August 1942, and the United States Navy heavy cruiser USS *Canberra* named in her honour in 1943. A new HMAS *Canberra* was later commissioned by the Royal Australian Navy in 1981.

P&O's chairman, Sir William Currie, had asked the Australian Prime Minister, Robert Menzies, to agree to the use of the name for his new ship. In the press release, which was datelined Canberra, Australia, Sir Donald Anderson explained the naming and the whole essence of the ship's being:

> The name has been chosen because it symbolises the part which P&O has played in the development of Australia's trade and commerce overseas for the last century and the growing importance in world affairs both of Australia and her capital city Canberra ...
>
> In the building of this new ship the P&O Company is assuming a continuance of British migration to Australia and the need for passenger ships to carry them in the most up-to-date conditions. A continuance of active migration is necessary for the company to justify the investment of £15,000,000 sterling in this ship. We estimate that a ship of this size and cost cannot be made to operate at a profit on the United Kingdom to Australia trade alone, but we look to obtaining adequate earnings by extending voyages across the Pacific. We believe that Australia is the keystone of the Pacific in development over the next fifty years. We have grown with and made a significant contribution to Australian development so far and intend, if we can, to continue to play our part in Australia's future.

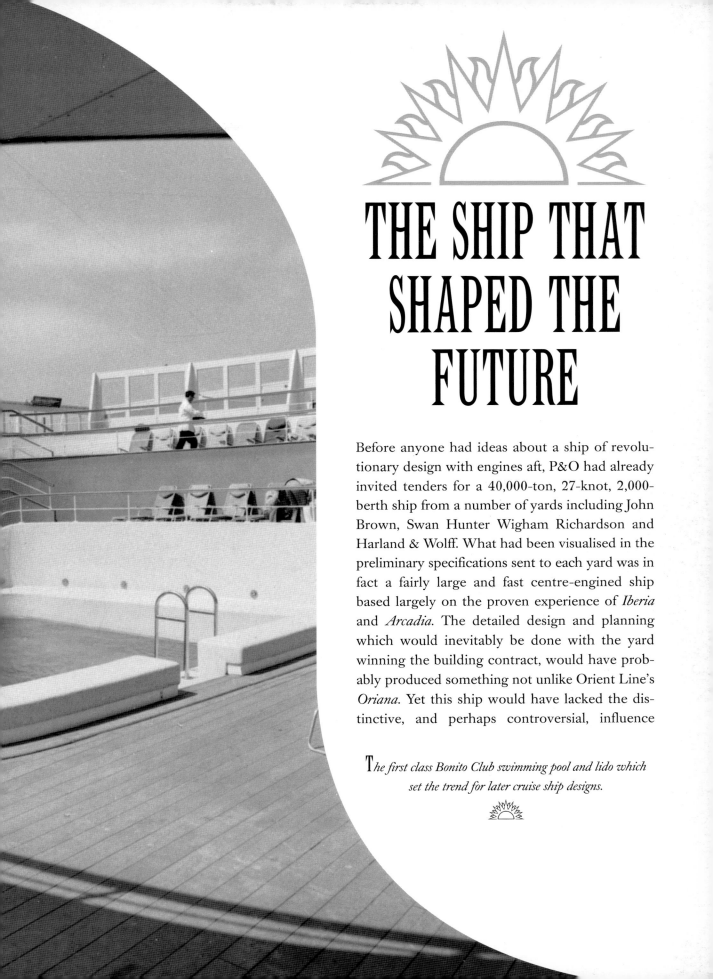

# THE SHIP THAT SHAPED THE FUTURE

Before anyone had ideas about a ship of revolutionary design with engines aft, P&O had already invited tenders for a 40,000-ton, 27-knot, 2,000-berth ship from a number of yards including John Brown, Swan Hunter Wigham Richardson and Harland & Wolff. What had been visualised in the preliminary specifications sent to each yard was in fact a fairly large and fast centre-engined ship based largely on the proven experience of *Iberia* and *Arcadia*. The detailed design and planning which would inevitably be done with the yard winning the building contract, would have probably produced something not unlike Orient Line's *Oriana*. Yet this ship would have lacked the distinctive, and perhaps controversial, influence

*The first class Bonito Club swimming pool and lido which set the trend for later cruise ship designs.*

which Orient Line's chief naval architect Charles Morris had brought to her as the crowning achievement of his long and distinguished career with the Line.

Progress in the new ship's planning in P&O's technical department, under their chief naval architect Arthur Temple, had, however, not escaped the eye of John West, an eager young naval architect working in the company's design office who had been involved in the planning of the oil tankers *Maloja* and *Mantua*. West was amazed that so large and prestigious a new ship was about to be built along such traditional and even old-fashioned lines. He thought about it, and in his spare time prepared an alternative plan for a liner based on far more modern ideas, no doubt somewhat inspired by the then recent example of *Southern Cross*.

West believed that as the 'human cargo' of the liner, passengers should be given the same pride of place in *Canberra*'s planning as were bulk cargoes of the tankers he had already been working on. In other words, the ship should be planned as far as possible around the infinitely more complex needs of her passengers, rather than merely accommodating them in the spaces left over after the machinery, bunkers, cargo and crew were all in place inside a conventional centre-engined hull. Naval architecture at the time was turning things around completely in the design of all types of cargo ships, to

*John West, the young naval architect whose inspired vision towards the future of shipping crucially influenced* Canberra's *shape.*

provide optimum carrying and handling of bulk cargoes. West's approach to *Canberra*'s design made the point that passengers, who are the most sophisticated and demanding of ships' cargoes (especially when things go wrong), needed to be served at least as well.

Applying the model of a supertanker with engines and crew-quarters aft, West was able in effect to create a closely-integrated 'floating hotel' block running through virtually the entire midships and forward parts of a sleek modern liner hull, with the machinery and funnels out of the way fully astern and with crew accommodation below and officers' quarters above, adjacent to the bridge. This had the added advantage of giving those responsible for the accommodation design the freedom to create modern hotel-type cabins and suites, on a straightforward and easily understood plan with varied and spacious public spaces which could take full advantage of the type of open planning gaining great popularity ashore. Properly done, this had the potential to create something with great public appeal.

However, this was to be no mere copy of *Southern Cross*, as *Canberra* was to be a ship of double the size and with the need to muster more than four times the power to give her the additional 6.5 knots speed. This meant that a far greater mass of machinery would have to be balanced into the stern end of a fine-lined hull

shape built for speed rather than bulk. Indeed, much work would have to be done to incorporate so fundamental a change in design, even at this early stage. Sceptical as Arthur Temple and his colleagues might have been about all this at first, they were nonetheless interested in what the twenty-seven year old prodigy was proposing.

The yards bidding for the contract were each asked to consider the possibilities of a ship with turboelectric machinery aft. In their response Vickers Armstrong noted that they had been asked by Orient Line to consider an aft-engined plan for *Oriana*, but that the conventional steam-turbine machinery which the owners wanted could not offer any advantages to the ship's overall layout. However, they thought the greater flexibility offered by a turboelectric installation would make the whole idea worth looking into.

P&O management saw in this new approach an opportunity to shed the line's public image of being rather dated in their design approach. Even their latest liners, *Iberia* and *Arcadia*, were in reality little more than larger renditions of the original '*Straths*' of the early 1930s. The interiors of these ships were in a time warp of 1930s oceanliner eclecticism which left P&O far behind even the subdued and understated modernity of all Orient Line ships' interiors since *Orion*'s introduction of contemporary styling and open planning in 1935. *Canberra* was thus not only to be a futuristic liner with engines aft, but was to be created as an 'artistic whole' by the largest team of designers ever to be assembled for the creation of a British ship. John West's ideas were in this regard somewhat symbolic of the company's new trading and commercial aspirations as well as being abjectly practical in terms of the new ship herself. West was extracted from his department and brought up into a management level to work on *Canberra*, ending up as assistant manager to Arthur Temple of the P&O-Orient Lines technical department, which had been renamed after P&O absorbed its younger subsidiary in 1960.

*At first* Canberra*'s plan bore a greater resemblance to* Oriana*'s layout with public rooms on the decks above the lifeboats.*

P&O expected great things of their new ship and of the many new ideas being introduced in her, and brought a great deal of pressure to bear on her designers and builders. As Sir Colin Anderson was later to comment:

> We have gone to great trouble to look for new solutions to old problems, employing the most advanced techniques we consider practical. We shall be disappointed if the *Canberra* does not transmit to her passengers the feeling, not in any sense of a revolution, but of a sharp break with all that is outdated and an imaginative surge into the future.

In 1957, when these decisions were being made, there were no specialist ships' interior architects as there are today. Accommodation tended to be decorated by contract furnishing firms or the shipyards themselves, often with shipping line

*An early artistic impression of the curvilinear exterior styling surrounding the first class pool.*

directors' wives having a hand in the choices of curtain materials, soft furnishings and artwork. The Raymond Loewy designed interiors of American Export Line's *Independence* and *Constitution* were notable exceptions to the general rule, as was the work done by Brian O'Rorke for Orient Line from his first commission in the 1930s to design *Orion*'s interiors right up to his work with *Oriana*.

Professional designers had to be hand-picked, largely on the basis of their reputation for flexibility and ingenuity in their work ashore. Sir Hugh Casson, whose diverse architectural, interior and industrial design work seemed entirely apropos, also had the unique experience of having designed the state apartments of the Royal Yacht *Britannia*. Sir Donald Anderson contacted him during *Canberra*'s very early planning, to co-ordinate a design team for the ship with John Wright and Barbara Oakley. Sir Hugh himself was responsible for the first class public rooms, while those of tourist class, along with the first class Crows Nest observation lounge fell within John Wright's jurisdiction. He had worked briefly with Brian O'Rorke for Orient Line, where he had been responsible for some special cabins and the tourist class library aboard *Orsova*. Barbara Oakley, who had previously advised P&O on colour schemes for *Arcadia* and *Iberia* was given responsibility for the cabins and the important connecting elements of the passageways, stairwells and deck lobbies.

So far as the difference between shore-side and shipboard work were concerned, Sir Hugh felt that some things were easier, but that one had to accept one's lot in the whole scheme of things:

> You don't have the problem of stopping the water coming in, which takes up half your time with a building. Here, all that's taken care of for you. And you have to get used to the idea of not being the most important person. You are given your space last, after the engines, and you have to make the best of what you have.

Sir Hugh was also asked to work with John West to provide *Canberra* with an element of exterior styling. His work here had the effect of softening the ship's lines, particularly in the details of the afterdeck openings and in the shape of the bridge and officer accommodation housing, as well as reducing any possible discord between new features such as the aft funnels and superstructure aerodynamics and the more traditionally nautical elements such as the hull lines prescribed by long-standing shipbuilding experience. It would blend the influences of convention and modernity with a tailored smoothness of line and form which would look 'right' in the public's eye.

Somebody wanted to promote *Canberra* to the public as 'the ship of the century', but Sir Donald felt that this was perhaps a little too presumptuous at a time when there was still forty years of history to be made before the millennium. He eventually acquiesced to 'The ship which shapes the future' as a more realistic sentiment of what was to be expected of '*Strathmost*'.

The amalgam of fresh and new ideas which came from this assembly of creative minds produced a ship of remarkable modern imagery and character. Both on the technical and artistic sides, *Canberra*'s creators were accorded an unusually free hand. This was then still possible, before the advent of cruise line 'brand marking' began to be imposed by the designer fleet identities now customary.

OVERLEAF

*Accommodation plans of* Canberra'*s four superstructure decks; note the court cabins forward.*

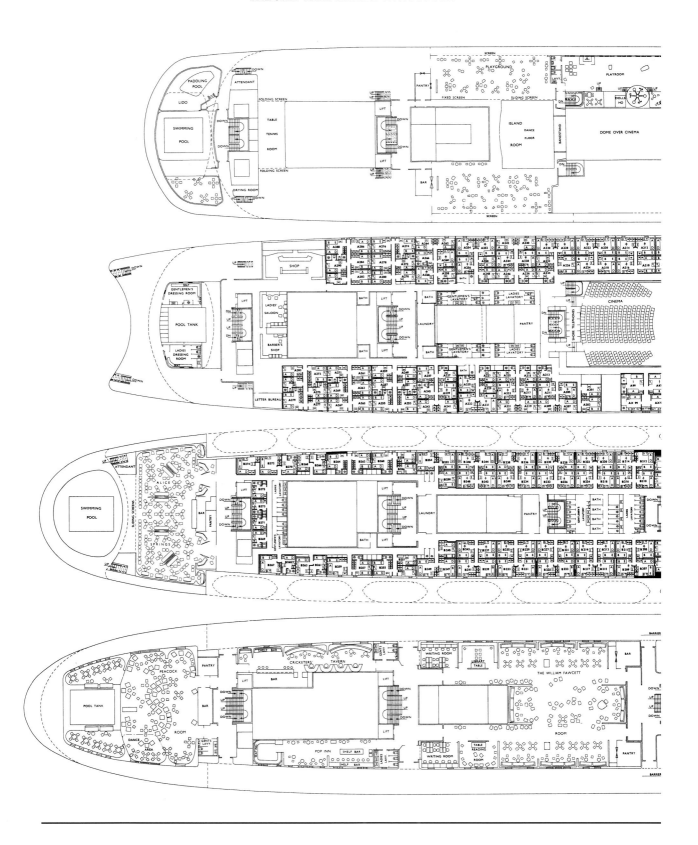

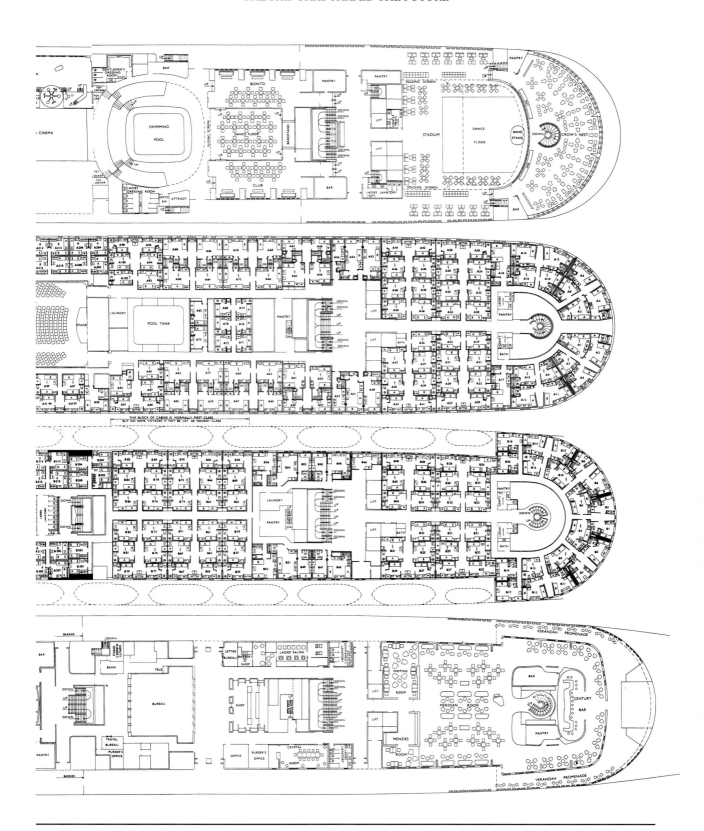

West's engines-aft ideas, together with the use of lightweight aluminium alloy in the superstructure and a nested lifeboat arrangement, formed the three key points which shaped the ship's design. Each of these was significant in optimising her passenger capacity within the size and capacity figures. With a compact tanker-style machinery installation concentrated as far aft as possible, much of the remaining internal space was left free and clear as the passengers' domain with a minimum of obstruction by the ship's technical workings. The aluminium superstructure's weight economy, and the extra cabin deck this allowed, along with the margins of stability and safety resulting from the nested lifeboat arrangement, combined to establish the basis of a truly remarkable ship.

Widely extolled as these features were to become in *Canberra*'s design, all of them had pedigrees of their own, to some extent or other having been already proven elsewhere, even if not previously applied on as large a scale. Yet none of them seems to have engendered the same trendsetting public appeal on their own as their combination in *Canberra*'s design has ultimately done.

Early examples of ships with their engines aft can be traced as far back as some early twentieth century examples of Canadian Pacific's Great Lakes steamers and a series of cargo/passenger packets for Matson Line's Hawaiian trade. However, these were done on a small scale, and used conventional machinery layouts which were merely moved as far aft as possible for various reasons. The French coastal ship *El Djezair* was among the first to demonstrate the possibilities of using a far more compact tanker-style steam plant arrangement. In steam-powered tankers it was a common space-saving measure for the boilers to be located fully astern and higher up above the propeller shafts, rather than forward of the turbines as was the more usual arrangement for passenger ships.

While this appears to have worked well in *El Djezair*, little was done in planning the ship's accommodation to take advantage of the freedom of layout it offered. Anyone travelling aboard this ship would have seen or experienced nothing that offered them anything new other than the peculiarly far aft position of her otherwise rather ordinary-looking funnel. However, since John West had studied shipbuilding in France at about the time of *El Djezair*'s planning, he had no doubt duly noted the further possibilities her design offered.

Three years later the same idea gained respectability in the eyes of the British public (who are not always keen on accepting anything foreign) when successfully tried on a larger scale with Shaw Savill's *Southern Cross*. Completed in 1955 by Harland & Wolff, she gave a far better impression of what could be done with the passenger accommodation layout of a modern aft-engined ocean liner. Her original interior layout, prior to many modifications in her later career, featured bright and airy rectangular public rooms and halls such as those found in hotels and resorts ashore, along with wide stairways and broad central corridors on her cabin decks which made it easy for passengers to find their way around the ship.

*Southern Cross* created considerable interest within the shipping and shipbuilding fields, with a number of proposals being put forward for other ships based on her design. One of these was for a 30,000-ton Atlantic liner in which the weight of the main engines aft was to be counterbalanced by amassing all the auxiliary machinery in the forward compartments, leaving the centre part of the ship clear for passenger accommodation. The problem of the funnels above the two machinery compartments being spaced too widely apart for a good visual appearance was solved by adding a third dummy stack housing an observation lounge amid-

*The unique electro-mechanical control console specifically designed for* Canberra's *power station-type engine plant.*

ships above the accommodation. Thus, externally at least any visual impact of such an unusual approach would be lost, but its advantages would, it was hoped, become apparent once inside the funnel-less centre part of the ship. For his proposed 120,000-ton North Atlantic behemoths of the 1950s, the American entrepreneur, Edgar Detwiler, opted to bank on the public appeal of the modernistic look of a ship remarkably sleek for her size with funnels at the extreme aft end of the superstructure. Ultimately, neither of these proposals materialised.

By the time *Canberra's* planning got underway a number of years later, Holland America Line's *Rotterdam* was taking shape with striking modern interiors which owed much of their outstanding layout to the two-thirds-aft location of her conventional steam machinery arrangement. Shaw Savill was then well enough assured of *Southern Cross's* success to build a second ship of similar design which was completed as *Northern Star* in June 1962, a year after *Canberra* was delivered.

John West took nothing for granted, and started from scratch in thinking every aspect of *Canberra's* design through. He looked as well to other developments in transport which showed similar new concepts:

> Whereas for some years it was a foregone conclusion that ships' engines were amidships, a car's engines were in the front and an aeroplane's engines on the wings, nowadays this is not necessarily so. Some cars have engines at the rear, others have them placed sideways in an attempt to use space with the utmost economy. Recent aircraft designs show high-powered jet engines at the rear. Ships now have machinery spaces in various positions – some aft, some amidships and some half-way between.

The same sort of daring that had gone into putting the jet pods of the French-made Sud Aviation *Caravelle* airliner aft and on the fuselage rather than the wings, and in Britain of turning the BMC Mini's engine sideways, would have to be brought to bear on *Canberra's* design. While there were other examples of aft-engined ships, both of passenger-carrying and specialist cargo types, the high performance demanded of the new P&O ship would demand that at least some of that experience would have to be rethought to make it work.

The eventual choice of machinery for *Canberra* packed a powerful industrial generating station-type steam turbine plant into the aft end of the ship's hull along with two pairs of doubled up electric motors capable of transmitting 42,500 shaft horsepower each to her propellers. This arrangement allowed for an extremely compact installation which would use a bare minimum of fore and aft space. Since the transmission of power to the propellers would be electrical rather than mechanical, as in a conventional marine-geared turbine installation, only the comparatively small drive motors would have to be lined up with the

propeller shafts allowing the turbines to be further aft than would otherwise have been possible.

In technical terms, *Canberra*'s machinery produced steam at high pressure from three Foster Wheeler ESD (External Superheat D type) boilers at 175,000 pounds per hour and a temperature of 969°F each. The steam plant offered an ample margin of redundancy as any two of the boilers would be able to supply sufficient steam for normal running, allowing the third to be descaled or otherwise maintained while at sea. A fourth smaller boiler with a capacity of 40,000 pounds per hour was also fitted to supply steam while in port. Steam was fed to the two main turbines which generated the electrical power to drive the propeller motors as well as the auxiliary engines to generate domestic power for lighting, air conditioning, cooking and other hotel or domestic services.

The main turbines were of a comparatively simple power station-type with a single cylinder containing eighteen rows of blading, as opposed to the usual triple-expansion marine turbine installation comprising separate high-, medium- and low-pressure turbines and a reverse-power unit. Mechanical governors allowed *Canberra*'s main turbines to be regulated between twenty-five and eighty-five per cent of their maximum speed for normal running conditions between 'dead slow' for port manoeuvring and 'full ahead' while underway at 27.5 knots. The top fourteen per cent provided a margin of safety which could be pushed for short spells only in dire necessity. From the generators driven by the main turbines electrical power was fed to the propeller drive motors at a maximum of 6,000 volts three-phase at 51.5 cycles or Hertz, similar to the voltages used in railway locomotives.

The motors used were of the 42-pole synchronous type, which allowed them to be controlled so that a constant relationship between the blade positions of the two propellers could be main-

tained. This was an important consideration in minimising vibration caused by the propellers, which in normal service turned at a maximum of 147rpm. *Canberra*'s installation actually used two motors for each shaft, offering the great flexibility of being able to run from one motor per shaft at lower speeds or of being able to switch the power source for each motor between the two main turbines. The ship could thus be run at about 22 knots with only one of the main turbines running. The switching arrangements also provided immediate full-astern power, a possibility not normally offered by conventional triple-expansion geared turbine machinery. Apart from its great operational flexibility, *Canberra*'s machinery has ultimately provided for remarkably smooth and quiet running throughout her service career.

Apart from the many outstanding features of *Canberra*'s internal layout and its architecture, as discussed later, one of the most compelling and attractive statements about her as a modern aft-engined ship was made externally by the appearance of her slender tanker-style stacks. Funnels have enormous potential to create a ship's image. They usually carry the colours and insignia of the line, making them an important mark of fleet identity and a significant element of the individual vessel's character. Owners were traditionally very cautious about tampering with the image of the conventional steamship funnel. It is for this reason that the image of the *Queen Mary*-style three-stacker remains to this day so deeply rooted in our culture that it still holds firm in the illustrations of children's books, commercial graphics and in the computer clip art and business icons which we continue to live with.

The Americans introduced the 'mack', a combination mast and stack, in a number of ships built during the late 1940s and through the 1950s. These appeared in the Del Line's late 1940s foursome of cargo/passenger *Dels*, but is perhaps best known for its use in Moore McCormack's *Argentina* and *Brasil* of a decade later. Everyone then probably still remembered how little enthusiasm there had been to follow the example of the East Asiatic Company's pioneering motorship *Selandia* with other funnel-less tonnage. Thus the *Dels*, *Argentina*, *Brasil* and others with macks were given large dummy funnels amidships to keep the aesthetics looking right. *Rotterdam* made a bold statement in 1959 with the distinctive tall and slender lines of her side-by-side 'goal post' funnels, standing against only a small extension of the superstructure amidships, housing the lift

*Canberra's powerful propellers as she sits in dry dock before launching; note the stern anchor which was removed early in her career.*

machinery and air conditioning plant rooms.

*Canberra*'s funnels were fashioned into twin tall tanker-style stacks which conveyed a popular impression of the modern oil ships which had influenced *Canberra*'s design in the first place. Supertankers then represented the oil industry's success and prestige, and its significant role in the burgeoning transport and automotive fields. Life Magazine, National Geographic and other popular periodicals had shown enough pictures of these behemoth tankers for most people to be able to pick up on their image as it would appear in *Canberra*'s styling. This at least made a statement of modernity and progress which everyone could understand far more readily than, for instance, *El Djezair*'s image of a ship with an ordinary funnel being further aft than perhaps one's traditional view of things says it ought to be.

*The tanker-style funnels which have perhaps been one of the most compelling aspects of the ship's profile throughout her life.*

Apart from any perceived supertanker imagery, *Canberra*'s aft funnel location and open deck spaces carried a real sense of something that once aboard could be understood and appreciated. The huge well laid-out expanse of topside open deck space, with an elaborate terraced swimming pool well, various sunbathing and sports areas separable one from the other with movable glass screens was unprecedented. It demonstrated, far more vividly than even the most open of public-room plans could, what was really possible in a jet- or space-age ocean liner planned without a brace of huge steamer funnels being in the way of everything else amidships. Those modern supertanker funnels were not merely to be seen from the quayside or at a distance from passing ships, but would stand above the playground they had made possible as a veritable icon of the ship's functional modernity.

*Canberra seen later in her career, showing the great extent of her 'topsides' open deck pools and lido areas.*

The slender mass of the funnels was visually counterbalanced by an aluminium forestructure housing the bridge and officers' quarters. The form of this, with its swept-back bridge wings, curvilinear windbreak fairings and passenger sun terraces could be seen and experienced during the time one spent aboard as an expression of contemporary aluminium shipbuilding. The aerodynamically inspired front of the superstructure proper was, however, something that could not be experienced by those aboard, since the bow deck was off limits to passengers. Compared with the earlier attempts at steamship streamlining, as in the rather heavy and contrived-looking steel bridge front of the French liner *Le Marseilles*, *Canberra*'s distinctly more fluid superstructure lines showed that the marine version of modern aircraft-type alloy construction offered great new design possibilities.

Proven precedents for the building of large aluminium upperworks on both *Oriana* and *Canberra* came from the fine examples of *United States* and *Bergensfjord*. A change from riveted to welded construction proportionally reduced the structural weight of these later ships in comparison with *United States*. However, the earlier examples showed few of the possibilities offered by these alloys for being worked into various modern aerodynamic-looking shapes adopted in *Canberra*.

An earlier modern precedent for nested lifeboats was to be found in the example of *Willem Ruys*. Here, the idea was applied against fairly conventional thinking on internal planning, mainly on the basis of optimising stability. Full advantage was also taken of the deck recess and the boats themselves to provide shade and protection from the tropical heat inside this ship's first class cabins which lacked air conditioning. However, this was otherwise somewhat at odds with the terraced arrangements of the ship's open decks and her interior layouts, with the public rooms concentrated on the upper decks.

Early plans for *Canberra*, before she had progressed much beyond the '*Strathmost*' stage, stressed a similar layout in which the public rooms, surrounded by an enclosed promenade, would have been sited above the lifeboat recesses. As detailed planning evolved it was realised that, since the boat recess would need a height of 20ft, it also made more sense to locate the public rooms at a level lower than usual. This would give the advantage of additional headroom where it would be needed rather than merely ending up with all cabins at this level having unusually high ceilings.

This placed *Canberra*'s Promenade Deck and main run of public rooms midway among the four principal cabin decks. Three levels higher up on Games Deck a versatile and informal second run of public spaces was planned with a greater emphasis on daytime activities around the open Sun Deck above and the first class swimming pool amidships. Three flights down from the Promenade Deck were the two dining rooms arranged in traditional liner style forward and aft of a central galley which served them both. The three separate runs of public spaces turned out to serve the ship in a similar manner to the major arteries of a town which bring together its various neighbourhoods. This scheme also diminished the passenger's perception of the ship's huge capacity and gave a 'local' feeling to the cabin areas.

Apart from their functions for entertainment and dancing, the Promenade Deck lounges would also be informal rendezvous points for passengers throughout the day. People would meet there for morning coffee after swimming or sunbathing on deck, a cold beer before lunch, afternoon tea following the matinée film show, bingo or a hand of bridge, cocktails before dinner and so on. Their central location would be well placed for bringing people together within easy reach of all the ship's

facilities, as one would only have to ascend or descend half the ship's total number of cabin decks to get to and from various activities.

So far as the public spaces themselves were concerned, *Canberra*'s funnels-aft layout allowed for large rectangular rooms and for a great deal of open planning, then very popular in all types of buildings ashore from private homes to schools, offices and resort hotels. The first class Meridian Lounge and Bonito Club were especially remarkable in this regard. The Meridian Lounge was created as the focal point of first class social activity as a suite of connected spaces arranged on a remarkably open plan giving an impression of infinite space.

*The elegant Meridian Lounge, with a sense of infinite space created by the 'corner-less' design.*

Its central lounge area was designed essentially as a room without inside corners. The solid walls aft separating the Meridian Lounge from the library and writing room were ended well short of the side walls, creating a seamless continuation of space from one area to the other. Forward, the Lounge was also carried on out of sight at either side, forming a loop which flowed around an enclosed service island, also housing the intimate Century Bar and the ship's magnificent spiral staircase.

The open planning was further emphasised by the curved form of the service island wall. This swept away to the extremities of the room at either side and to the foot of the spiral staircase at the centre. Around the turns from the main room, the entrances to the service pantries were discreetly concealed within gentle 'folds' in the contour of the wall. At the opposite side, four absolutely flush wall panels opened up other folds, revealing access

to the dark and intimate Century Bar within. Sir Hugh Casson's approach to designing this space no doubt drew on his experience in the early 1950s where he pulled off a similar trick of open planning, albeit on a much smaller scale, in his design for the state apartments of the Royal Yacht *Britannia*. There a fairly simple arrangement of wide folding doors allowed the drawing room, ante-room and main entrance to be effectively combined for large state functions. In these spaces, along with the much smaller private sitting rooms for HM the Queen and HRH the Duke of Edinburgh, an added impression of spaciousness was gained by using rounded rather than square corners.

The Bonito Club and its adjoining swimming pool on Games Deck, also designed by Sir Hugh, likewise stressed open planning, although of a more informal nature than in the Meridian Lounge. This was intended to be a versatile multipurpose area which would serve as a lido café during the daytime and as a plush ballroom in the evenings. The pool lido was joined with the Bonito Club itself by means of a retractable glass wall which could be lowered vertically out of sight into the floor. With this out of the way, the outdoor lido and the inside dance floor became a continuous indoor/outdoor area. The impression of openness and spaciousness was further enhanced by the series of terraces aft of the pool leading up to the Sun Deck above.

The pool lido would effectively be extended into the room during the daytime when, for instance, the Bonito Club could be used for the lunchtime pool-side buffet. In the evenings the roles were reversed, with the dance floor flowing outside, encompassing the lido. The Bonito Club's

*The melding of* Canberra*'s indoor and outdoor worlds at the Bonito Club and pool as seen here after nightfall.*

*The Century Bar seen as a shaded oasis of intimacy even during the bright daylight hours in the tropics.*

teak dance floor/indoor lido was originally surrounded on the remaining three sides by a solid teak balustrade separating it from raised seating areas to either side and a bandstand forward.

There were two additional ideas for this area that unfortunately never materialised. The first was a retractable glass dome covering the entire swimming pool recess at the Sun Deck level. The other was a movable floor section, concealed beneath the lido, which would have allowed the dance floor to be extended covering the pool. Both features would have added to the area's versatility and, at that time, been of great interest in themselves. No doubt they were foregone out of concern both over their technical complexity and their cost.

Sir Hugh's approach to the decoration of his spaces and in co-ordinating the theme of the entire ship stressed crisp, clean modern lines and forms with a sense of warmth and understated elegance. In his own words:

Throughout the first class in *Canberra*, for instance, ceilings are almost universally white and kept as flat and unbroken as it is technically

possible. The rubber floors of staircases, alley-ways, entrances and the carpet of the principal public room (the Meridian Lounge) are the rich blue-green of the Pacific. Walls are almost uni-versally of dark smoky woods – Persian walnut, Indian laurel – or else white. Bright colours – flames, pinks and oranges – are either (as in the Bonito Club) kept concealed by day and brought out only at night, or confined to areas (such as the cinema) untouched by daylight. Satin silver metalwork, opalescent glass-fibre, polished glass and natural leather and cane almost complete the range of materials used in these areas. In the tourist areas, by contrast, where spaces are larger and the required atmos-phere is to be less discreetly quiet, colour and textures are used boldly and generously, with

*The spiral staircase which has remained one of the ship's most outstanding architectural features over the years.*

gay mosaics and richly translucent gold-foil panels, murals – one more than 200ft long – fountains, woods as pale as willow and as dark as rosewood, or stained to a strong stinging blue. Ceilings are sculpted to subtle forms. Throughout both areas the lighting has been flexibly devised to change to meet the mood of the moment or the time of day. Linked by the blue-green floors and predominantly white walls of the alleyways and the cabins, large and small, mostly in natural woods set against white walls, where vivid colours are kept to occasional and very carefully considered points of interest.

Apart from the Meridian Lounge and Bonito Club, there were two other very special interiors created by Sir Hugh. The spiral staircase, which connected the Meridian Lounge with the Crow's Nest observation lounge on Games Deck, was undoubtedly one of *Canberra*'s most dramatic architectural features. The stairs rose through three decks within a large cylinder clad entirely in the same smoky wood as the Meridian Lounge. The white terrazzo marble stairtreads were suspended from deep aluminium-clad balustrades. Indirect fluorescent lighting concealed in the soffit of the outer balustrade provided the only source of illumination. The effect was both dramatic and unusual, with much of the light being reflected upwards from the steps themselves, making them appear to float freely in its glow.

*Canberra*'s dining rooms, located on E deck, were designed as entirely inside spaces without portholes, despite being full-width rooms well above the water line. The first class Pacific dining

room was particularly remarkable for its distinctive lighting scheme which created entirely different characters, bright and cheerful during the daytime, then subdued and romantic during the evening dinner hours. The brighter daytime scheme came from ceiling fixtures and from back-lit translucent wall panels. The overhead illumination was from clustered fibreglass cylinders of varying diameters and lengths. These had the appearance of stylised stalactites covering the centre part of the ceiling, above a shallow floor recess of corresponding dimensions. The surrounding ceiling was slightly lower, and the only one on the ship to be clad in the same dark wood as the walls. Here the overhead light source consisted of narrow recessed fluorescent strips in extending beams. Continuous back-lit wall panels along both sides of the room radiated a medium-intensity ambient glow like warm sunlight filtered through Japanese-style woven straw screens. This effect was produced by using textured fibreglass.

*The Pacific Dining Room illuminated as it has been throughout* Canberra's *career for breakfast, lunch and tea service.*

*The Pacific Dining Room in its more intimate dinner hour appearance with the table lanterns illuminated.*

*The Alice Springs Lounge with its wicker furniture, evocative perhaps of an informal lifestyle awaiting emigrant passengers in the Australian outback.*

The 'dinner hour' mood was achieved by darkening the wall panels and switching to small electric lanterns on each table. Fluorescent 'wall washers' at the foot of the wall screens were used along with reduced ceiling lighting to give the room a warm low level ambient glow.

Both lighting moods were effective, and the visual impact of switching from one to the other dramatic to say the least. *Canberra* was the first British ship to use so elaborate a lighting scheme. It took some convincing of the owners on Sir

Hugh's part, as they feared that the crew would simply disregard his 'theatrical lighting plot'. Stewards are in the business of serving passengers rather than worrying about mood lighting, therefore they might be inclined to keep all lights switched on to make their work easier. Proof of the success of the Pacific Dining Room's lighting plot lies in the fact that it, and the entire room's decoration, have remained very little changed throughout the ship's long life.

John Wright had *Canberra*'s two largest spaces, the William Fawcett (later the Ocean Room) and Island rooms in his tourist class design domain. However, as the greater numbers of tourist passengers would in effect each have less elbow room in these, Wright cleverly used partitions to diminish

*The ever-popular Cricketer's Tavern which has
always been at the centre of life
aboard* Canberra.

the chance of creating a dreary impression of vast overcrowded halls. His approach was to give these and several smaller rooms each a character of their own that would attract people with different interests who would "identify" themselves with particular themes. The William Fawcett Room was to be an up-to-date adaptation of the old winter garden or palm court idea, which would appeal to families for daytime use while the Peacock Room (later to be renamed Neptune's), with its curved walls and alcoves, was intended to attract quieter and perhaps more elderly passengers.

Like the Bonito Club, the Island Room was a dual-purpose daytime and evening multifunction area. Less sophisticated than its first class counterpart, it lacked any direct access to the tourist pools,

one farther aft and one two decks below. It was arranged with movable glass walls which both divided it into several sections for various activities and opened it up along either side of the ship as a combined indoor/outdoor space which could be enjoyed in the tropics.

John Wright also created the Cricketer's Tavern, which ultimately proved to be one of *Canberra*'s best-loved and most enduring rooms. This long and narrow space, with somewhat the proportions of a railway carriage, was entirely

designed around a cricket theme. Sir Colin Cowdrey, the famous England cricketer, was consulted on the decoration, which included specially-commissioned life-size portraits of cricket immortals such as W G Grace, Sir Donald Bradman, Sir Learie Constantine and K S Ranjitsinhji. The room's decoration also included a twine-wound bar grip fashioned in the manner of a bat handle, while its inner wall opposite the windows was decorated with genuine cricket items including bats, balls, gloves, stumps and club caps.

*Canberra*'s interiors were timelessly modern and appropriate to the era without appearing avant-garde, garish or even faddish. Yet the geometry of these spaces was tempered by the metre of the ships structure. Large spaces such as the Meridian and William Fawcett rooms were designed around the periodic intrusion of the web frames at their outer sides in a manner suggesting, subliminally at least, the ship's structural compartmentation. The open decks beyond these rooms' windows were suffused to the unquestionably nautical milieu of the steamship promenade, with its teak planking, canvas deck chairs, open metal railings and varying seascapes. There could be no mistaking the special sense of place which being aboard ship offers.

In connection with designing the hairdressing salons, Sir Hugh Casson wanted to know if ladies preferred to get their hair washed from in front or behind. Unable to get a conclusive answer from Lady Casson, his secretary or other ladies who happened to be around, Sir Donald canvassed his office staff, and in the absence of any real consensus of opinion, pointed out that washing from behind might cause dizziness on account of a ship's movement with passengers facing the ceiling, but that it was preferable to washing from the front as there was less chance of spoiling ladies' make-up. Another question concerned the amount of damage to floor and deck coverings to be expected from stiletto-heeled women's shoes – Orient Line's Charles Morris had particularly strong views on this particular hazard.

Guy R Fountain, founder and chairman of the Tannoy Group of Companies, wrote concerning the firm's role in supplying the public address system and other sound equipment to *Canberra*. He felt that, as the trade name 'Hoover' had become a generic English-language verb for using a vacuum cleaner, 'Tannoy' should appear on the audio switch plates in *Canberra*'s cabins in place of the word 'Broadcast'. Sir Donald declined with thanks. The marine superintendent wanted to have chilled drinking water piped to all cabins, raising questions concerning the arrangement of washbasin taps. A double faucet was to be fitted at one side of the basin while the single tap for drinking water would be on the other.

*Canberra*'s 2,238 passengers were to be accommodated in 814 cabins, ranging from four deluxe suites and eight smaller suites, through doubles and singles to interchangeable cabins which could be booked as first or tourist class, others which converted from four-berth rooms without private facilities to doubles with their own en-suite bathrooms and finally to the large numbers of double and four-berth rooms which would be the lifeblood of the ship's Australian emigrant trade.

A distinctive feature of *Canberra* was her court cabins, which were a clever trick of planning devised to bring daylight into what would otherwise have been inside cabins. The secondary passages off the main fore-and-aft corridors which give access to the outer cabins were widened at each successive pair of cabins to provide 'borrowed light' to the inner rooms from windows in the ship's side at the end of the passage, which

*One of the courts with settee and coffee table encouraging passengers to use the space as an informal gathering place.*

itself formed a common court shared by the four to eight cabins it accessed.

This too was not an entirely new idea. Layouts of similar concept were first proposed in the late 1920s by the noted American naval architect George G Sharp. Only limited application was made of this system in Sharp's own work, with its use of space being perhaps considered rather extravagant for the ships in which it was tried. However, the Italian-flag Cosulich Line's *Saturnia* of 1927 adopted the idea quite extensively, although it was not repeated in later Italian liners.

In the late 1940s Sharp himself made another strong pitch for the idea, feeling that it had great merit in the large air-conditioned ships which he foresaw for the future. He presented plans of his 'air-light' arrangement as hypothetical alternatives to three existing ships including P&O's *Himalaya*, Furness Line's *Queen of Bermuda* and United States Lines *Manhattan/Washington*, showing that the system was workable without loss of passenger capacity.

The inspired variation of this layout employed by John West and his design team in *Canberra*, using modern lightweight materials with a compact and efficient plan, achieved a remarkable sense of contemporary elegance and serviceability. The sense of openness, both in the cabins and the courts, offered passengers something very tangible as being modern and up-to-date.

Rather than following the then still prevalent carpenter-styling of cabins aboard contemporary

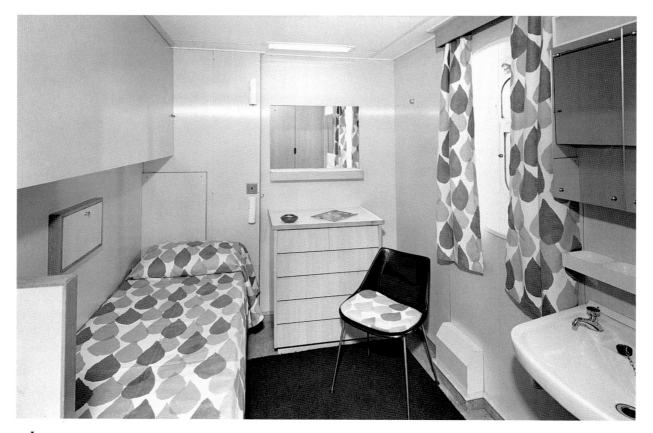

A *simple lower-grade tourist cabin with an impression of space created by built-in fixtures and light colours.*

British ships such as *Southern Cross* and *Transvaal Castle*, *Canberra*'s accommodation reflected the more up-to-date character of the latest American, Italian and Scandinavian ships. Their clean-lined modernity and functionality belonged more to technologically-inspired design ideals of the modern long-distance railway sleeping-car suite or even the airliner interior, than to the past era of the ocean liner. The rooms were finished with attractive but hard-wearing Perstorp wall coverings rather than paint and varnishes, and they featured the pullman efficiency of built-in furniture and fittings along with up-to-date lighting and other services as meticulously thought out as

those of the Boeing 707 and Douglas DC-8 airliner interiors. In the forward end of A and B decks a radial court cabin plan was used inside the semi-circular superstructure front, overcoming the usual shortcomings of layout inside the rounded ends of ships' decks.

Barbara Oakley, who was responsible for the detailed planning of *Canberra*'s cabins found that doing these rooms, which she described as being shaped like 'pieces of cheese', was something of 'a Chinese puzzle'.

There were also some ingenious emigrant cruise rooms which converted from a four-berth basic unit to a room for two with en- suite toilet in much the same way as a railway compartment could be adapted between daytime and night-time service. Even at this mundane level, *Canberra*'s layout and interior design followed the

airlines' philosophy of creating an on-board environment which celebrated the wonder, excitement and romance of travel, as well as reassuring the passenger of his or her safety and well-being within the technically-devised environment of a mobile body or vehicle.

Following on her earlier work with P&O, Barbara Oakley was also responsible for the colour schemes of *Canberra*'s accommodation stating:

> As with most ships, one of the most acute problems of designing the cabins of the *Canberra* is to make the maximum use of the space available. White walls seem to create greater illusions of space than coloured ones; thus with white predominant we needed dark carpets and deep colours on the furniture to make the rooms come alive and give them character.
>
> We have kept the vivid colours – emerald green, amethyst, brilliant red, and tangerine – for the cushions and chairs, and by keeping these important highlights to small areas we hope not only to increase their dramatic effect, but also to go on replacing them when the colours become drab or dated.
>
> Although fashions in colours do not change quite as quickly as hemlines, there is no doubt that by some curious telepathy we find ourselves drawn to entirely different colours as the years go by. Consequently no schemes are likely to last more than a fraction of the life of the ship, and our object has been to create the classical bones on which to drape delectable fabrics – in its own generation.

With *Canberra*'s engineering, structural and interior design having been created as a whole, she had already the makings of a remarkably successful ship, even before her keel was laid. What remained to be seen in the ship that would finally emerge was whether this amalgam of creativeness had the right public appeal.

## *CANBERRA*
### SPECIFICATIONS AS BUILT

| | |
|---|---|
| Length, overall | 820' |
| Beam, moulded | 102' |
| Draught, maximum | 32'6" |
| Gross Register Tonnage | 44,807 tons |
| Maximum trial speed | 29.27 knots |
| Service speed | 27.5 knots |
| Propulsion | Turbo-electric, twin screw |
| Number of Decks | 14 |
| Passenger capacity | 2,238 |
| Crew | 960 |
| Cargo capacity | 150,000cu ft |

# 'MEAT AND DRINK TO THE ISLAND'

The news that *Canberra* was to be built at Harland & Wolff was received with great jubilation in Belfast. The Musgrave Yard on Queen's Island had been laid out for, and had grown and prospered with, a steady diet of building passenger-carrying ships. White Star Line's iron-hulled *Germanic*, whose service life spanned an incredible sixty years, and their steel-built *Oceanic* were among the yard's best-known ships of the late nineteenth century. After the turn of the century came *Olympic*, *Titanic* and *Britannic*, as well as Union Castle's *Capetown Castle*. Royal Mail's *Austurias* and *Alcantara*, Union Castle's *Carnarvon Castle* and White Star's last Belfast-built ships

*Finally completed,* Canberra *manoeuvres in the King George V Dock in Southampton before running her sea trials in May 1961.*

*Britannic* and *Georgic* all represented Harland & Wolff's progress in the then emerging world of the motor ship. Royal Mail's *Andes*, which had only gone into commercial service after the Second World War, was regarded by many to be one of the most handsome British tropical liners ever to have been built at Queen's Island – or anywhere else for that matter.

P&O's connection with Queen's Island was one of the longest, going all the way back to the iron steamer *Rosetta,* completed in 1880. Their first ships of over 20,000 tons, *Mooltan* and *Maloja* of 1923, were also Belfast-built, as was *Canberra*'s immediate predecessor *Iberia*.

Apart from the many liners, large and small, built by Harland and Wolff since 1861, there had

*A model of* Canberra *showing her at a fairly advanced design stage, but before the wind fairings were added to her bridge decks.*

been the inevitable disappointments. White Star's 1,000-foot *Oceanic* was never completed due to the Great Depression in the 1930s. The Cunard *Queens* and a number of other prestigious ships had been built 'across the water' in English and Scottish yards. (In fact, *Parthia* was the only Cunard liner ever to have been built at Queen's Island). Many in Belfast had feared that this progressive new P&O liner with engines aft and a huge futuristic-looking superstructure might also pass them by.

For many in Belfast the *Canberra* contract represented, quite apart from any aspirations of prestige and glory, the basic bread-and-butter matter of continued employment. Passenger-ship building has always been a very labour-intensive enterprise, more so then than now, requiring a great many skilled workers in numerous finishing trades. With as many as several thousand tradespeople working during the fitting out stages of a large passenger ship, Harland & Wolff's contribution to the economy of Queen's Island and Belfast was indeed significant. The maximum 3,500 jobs which *Canberra*'s building

would either sustain or create amounted to about half of the yard's maximum workforce.

As one seasoned worker, an 'Islander' of the fifth generation in his family to work for Harland & Wolff, commented to the yard's deputy managing director, Dr Denis Rebbeck, in early 1957, 'Doctor, this new P&O liner will be meat and drink the Island'.

After the building contract was signed, there followed months of detailed planning and preparation work which finalised her precise form and plan. Literally miles of blueprint paper were filled with the meticulously hand-drawn plans, schematics and diagrams.

The Yarrow-Admiralty Research Department was given permission by the Admiralty to advise P&O as consultants on the design and building of *Canberra*'s machinery, based on their experience with high-performance propulsion systems for the Royal Navy. The machinery itself was to be built at Rugby by British Thomson Houston (later to become part of AEI) a company specialising in stationary power-generating machinery. Extensive research and calculations had to be done to ascertain the expected levels of vibration so that the necessary structural stiffening could be provided. The weight of the installation was a sensitive matter, which had to be worked out to the last fraction of a ton in view of its extremely far aft location aboard the ship.

Models of *Canberra*'s hull were tested in the National Physical Laboratory's towing tank at St. Albans to determine the merits of such things as a bulbous bow and whether or not a twin skeg stern and exposed propeller shafting would help optimise performance. A bulbous forefoot, quite large for the time, was eventually adopted with a conventional stern and exposed propeller shafts supported by carefully-shaped 'A' brackets. Models were wind-tunnel tested by the laboratory's aero-

*Canberra's bulbous bow which would add the necessary stability and buoyancy to the hull's fine-lined form at the waterline.*

dynamics division to ascertain the superstructure lines that would offer the least wind resistance, to arrange screens and wind breaks that would minimise the effects of high winds on the open decks and to find a funnel shape that would keep smoke and soot away from the swimming pools and lido decks. Some very futuristic ideas were tried,

*The aluminium upperworks taking shape, showing A, the funnel casing; B, Sun Deck; C, Games Deck children's area; D, Games Deck pool; E, 'A' Deck; F, 'B' Deck lido; G, Alice Springs pool.*

including two versions of an oblique fin type, looking like those used more recently in Adnan Kashoggi's private yacht. Apart from being far too avant garde in those days before *Carnival*'s gullwinged funnels, they simply didn't work as well as the tall slender stacks which have ultimately created *Canberra*'s distinctive image.

At the same time, the yard was prepared for her building. The channel in front of Number 14 slipway, where *Canberra* would be launched, and the fitting berth at which she would be completed had to be dredged. The Belfast Harbour Commission would also have to deepen the Victoria Channel through which *Canberra* would pass to run her sea trials and eventually make her delivery voyage.

The workforce had to be assembled with several hundred shipwrights who would build the hull and superstructure working alongside the thousands of craftsmen from various trades who completed and fit out the ship's inner workings and accommodation. New equipment was needed for welding aluminium alloys and yard workers had to be trained in the special techniques involved. The materials themselves, thousands of tons of steel and aluminium, had to be ordered and their deliveries scheduled. The huge propeller shaft brackets and shaft bossings would come from Germany, while the aluminium radar mast was to be manufactured as a whole in Norway by an aviation equipment-maker.

Later on, a constant stream of other items, ranging from boilers, turbines and condensers,

through two pairs of stabilisers, numerous air-conditioning plants, twenty-four lifeboats and davits, two sets of custom made lateral-boom cargo transporters, baggage handling equipment, acres of Swedish-made plastic laminate wall coverings, miles of Burma teak deck-planking, lift machinery, galley fittings and a printing press, down to lounge and cabin furniture, baby cots, bed and table linen, glassware, cutlery and crockery, all had to be ordered, with their arrivals at Queen's Island scheduled no earlier or later than precisely when they would be needed.

It was not until 23 September 1957 that the first section of *Canberra*'s keel was laid on the inclined ways of Number 14 slipway. As the very first manifestation of a new ship's being, keel layings were events which attracted little attention beyond the shipyard itself. It was the launching which was the real birth rite, when, as a recognisable body, a ship was named and christened in her first contact with her natural element of the sea. Indeed no greater honour could be bestowed on a ship than that the lady chosen officially to name her and trigger her launch should be a reigning monarch or a national head of state.

Sir Donald Anderson had been courting Buckingham Palace since early 1959 for the favour of Queen Elizabeth II's presence in Belfast to launch *Canberra*, as she had done Britain's first aft-engined ship *Southern Cross* a few years earlier. After initially agreeing to the March 1960 engagement, it later turned out that the Queen would then be in the latter stages of pregnancy with Prince Andrew, and that she would have to decline. The honour fell then to Dame Pattie Menzies, wife of Australia's Prime Minister, Sir Robert Menzies.

On 16 March 1960, Australia's genteel First Lady stood before the great new white ship which was to symbolise Australia's bright and prosperous future. Adding a special touch to the ceremony, she first pinned a sprig of white heather to the ribbons holding the bottle of Australian wine with which the ship was to be christened. The heather had been sent to her in Australia by P&O's chairman, Sir William Currie, so that it had already made the 22,000-mile round trip that embraced the new ship's service.

With the words, 'I name this ship *Canberra*. May God protect her and all who sail in her', Dame Pattie pressed the button to liberate the bottle, which shattered over the hull plating, and release the four half-ton launching triggers holding the ship in place before her. As thousands of shipyard workers and visitors cheered and horns and whistles blared all around on that chilly and overcast Thursday afternoon, *Canberra*'s bulbous bow forefoot slid away from the launch platform. In the time-span of a minute, 15,100 tons of steel and aluminium slid down the inclined building ways between the two columns of shipyard cranes which had brooded over the building of her hull and superstructure for the past year and a half. As the last drag chain was slipped from the ship, she floated free for the first time, while falling into the charge of a small fleet

*The launch party assembling on March 16 1960. Dame Pattie Menzies is seen at centre right in the calf-length coat.*

*Canberra takes to the water from slipway 14.*

of tugs which would pull and nudge her alongside the nearby Thompson Wharf where she would spend another year in construction and fitting out.

The traditional launch which *Canberra* was given that afternoon was an ancient and honoured rite of human technical achievement with a magnificence all its own, unmatched by any other celebration of P&O's accomplishments. Such launches breathed life into the largest movable objects created by civilisation in a way that was appropriately spectacular and awe-inspiring. In the eyes of those who still cherish memories of such occasions, today's shipbuilding has lost a significant piece of its proud heritage to the mundane process of merely floating a new hull off the level bottom of a drydock.

As work on *Canberra* progressed, countless details had to be worked out. Port facilities at Southampton and Sydney were modernised to handle her larger numbers of passengers. Other ports at which she would call along the way needed to be surveyed to ensure that they could accommodate her greater depth, so that berthing plans could be made. Scheduling had to be worked out to fit *Canberra* and *Oriana* in with the other sixteen ships in P&O's fleet, and so that their divergent routes and services would all meet at the

One of the lateral-boom cargo transporters in an extended position ready to lower its platform to the quayside.

right times and places and would not get in each other's way at other times. This meant integrating the new 27.5-knot superships, capable of making 650 nautical miles a day, with the smaller and earlier generation 22.5-knot 540-mile-a-day post-war vessels and the remaining pre-war 18.5-knot tonnage which were only able to steam 430 miles over 24 hours.

In Carron, Scotland, a Rolls Royce was hauled back and forth on an aluminium platform a couple of feet off the floor of a factory. It was the final test for one of the twin retractable lateral-boom cargo transporters before being shipped off to Northern Ireland for installation in *Canberra*. If the new-fangled device could handle a Rolls, it would easily handle other cars and whatever else passengers

might want to take with them. These alloy telescoping baggage conveyors were important aspects of the ship's design which allowed for so large a superstructure to be built without having to make provision for the usual hatches and cargo cranes. *Canberra*'s boilers were lit for the first time and a trial run-up made of her 6,000-volt main

Canberra's *officers assembled for her maiden voyage. Back row, left to right: J G Clarke, First Officer; T Sutton, Third Officer; N Thawley, Fourth Officer; D G Black, Jr First Officer; D J Perry, Third Officer. Front row, left to right: G E Howe, Nav. Officer; M R Prowse, Staff Capt; G A Wild, Captain; R A Game, Ch. Officer; M V N Bradford, Snr First Officer.*

generators, while topsides twenty-four fibreglass lifeboats which had newly arrived from Ashford were hoisted aboard in counterbalanced Welin-Maclachlan under-deck davits specially made for *Oriana* and *Canberra*.

Meanwhile, as bookings were being taken around the world for *Canberra*'s first voyages, her officers and crew were being assembled. Geoffrey Alan Wild, the fifty-seven year old captain whose most recent commands included *Strathaird* and *Arcadia*, was appointed as *Canberra*'s master in April 1961. During the final stages of her building he took up residence at the nearby Crawfordsburn Inn on Belfast Lough, while he supervised his new ship's preparations for her sea trials and delivery to P&O. Dressed in a business suit he had the look of a dapper executive of the builders, the owners or

perhaps one of the classification people from Lloyd's as he took his first lunch in *Canberra*'s then unfinished dining room. It would not be until only a few days before her departure from Belfast that he would move into the master's suite aboard and dress in his gold-braided uniform for the first time aboard *Canberra*.

Wild's appointment to *Canberra* would reunite him with an old friend, Purser Leonard Samuel Warren, from his early days with P&O. The two served together in 1930 aboard their first ship, *Ranpura*, running P&O's passenger and cargo service to India and China. Wild was a junior officer and Warren a purser's clerk. While remaining firm

*A party from* Canberra's *Indian crew prepare to lower the rope 'fender' used to protect the ship's hull for transit of the Panama Canal.*

friends, both men pursued their separate careers with the Line before *Canberra* was to bring them back together in the line of duty. When Wild was appointed as captain, Warren had already been 'standing by' the ship for some months, one of his main responsibilities being the laying in of the vast quantities of supplies of one sort and another that she would need when she went into service. As administrative chief of the ship's hotel and commercial workings, his role would be of primary importance to the ship's master, and his old friend, Geoffrey Wild.

Chief engineer John Skakle, who had been promoted from the same position in *Strathnaver*, had been at Queen's Island with *Canberra* since January 1960, before she was launched, while chief chef, Donald Glavin, was busy during the ship's last weeks in Belfast procuring the stores that he would need for feeding some 3,000 passengers and crew during her trials, delivery and first months in

service. Meanwhile, John Herbert, a young apprentice baker applied for a position aboard *Canberra* after reading an article about the ship's ultra-modern, electrically-powered bakeries in a trade magazine. He got the job, and has remained with the ship ever since, where he has worked his way to the top as chief baker.

The senior officers would be supported by other officers, petty officers, deck and engine ratings, hotel staff, laundrymen and entertainers who would bring the head count of *Canberra*'s 'palace guard' to 960 souls. Among these would be 48 Pathan and Punjabi engine ratings, 78 seamen recruited in Bombay and 320 Goanese hotel staff for the purser's department. Asian crews had been serving in P&O ships for generations since the Line first established their routes to India and the Far East in the 1840s. Sarfaraz Khan, appointed as Serang (who serves as a leading hand or bosun) in charge of the Asian engine-room crew, embodied this tradition in his forty-one years of continuous service with P&O. His two sons had followed him, the eldest serving as Serang in another P&O ship and the youngest having served under him aboard *Iberia*. Sarfaraz Khan was awarded a British Empire Medal in the 1961 New Year's Honours List, and the Line had honoured his long service with an appointment to their newest ship. A separate Serang would head the Indian deck crew, while the Goanese leading hand would hold the position of chief pantryman.

Thus was woven the fabric of *Canberra*'s crew family, who would take her from the hands of her designers and builders into service and the care of what would become an ever-growing worldwide family of loyal passengers. It is a sort of 'changing of the guard' in the life of any new ship as the yard workers hand her over to the crew who take her to sea. After having gone to work aboard *Canberra* for months, even years, the prospect of saying goodbye

*The builder's plate which bespeaks the ship's origins. The radome above is a later addition to* Canberra*'s electronic navigational equipment.*

to the great new ship would be sad to say the least.

For many, including John Erskine, a fifty-six year old joiner with forty years experience at Harland & Wolff to his credit, the prospects were worse than that; 'We all may get laid off after this one', he told a London reporter. Another turned his back to the ship as she was leaving Belfast and said, 'I wouldn't mind so much if she was coming back'. The 'meat and drink' which *Canberra*'s building had brought to the Island for the four years of her gestation were running out, especially for those in the finishing trades on which passenger ships are so reliant.

Some would find jobs in the local building trades, others would have to 'cross the water' in search of work, while a few would, like *Canberra* herself, depart Belfast altogether. Boilermaker William Lucas and welders Billy Cadoo and Francis Bingham, each with their young families, would sail on the maiden voyage of the ship they had helped build, bound for new lives 'down under' where the three men had jobs lined up at a shipyard in Whyalla, South Australia. Bingham spoke of the yard and ship with affection as he and his family prepared to leave Belfast:

> Of course I'll regret leaving the old shipyard, for which you develop quite an affection over the years. I hope the place I'm going to, and the gaffers, are as good, for Harland & Wolff have been good employers. But I'm very happy and honoured to sail to a new life on the *Canberra*. She is more than just a number to us shipyard-men. She is a household name in every ship-yardman's home in Belfast. Even the kids in the street know there's a *Canberra* being built.

With the experience of building so prestigious and modern a ship as *Canberra* under their belts, Harland & Wolff management were hopeful of a shot at the contract to build the new Cunard *Queen* then being planned. Prospects for large passenger ship contracts were otherwise doubtful, with the reality of future business clearly lying in the field of specialist cargo tonnage.

When *Canberra* left Harland & Wolff in a light fog at 10:00hrs on Saturday 29 April 1961 she was given a tumultuous send-off by the people of Belfast. As various commands and announcements could be heard from the ship's public address system, a crane swung the last of her gangways ashore, a puff of white smoke appeared from one of her funnels and the mooring lines splashed into the dark water. The London tug *Southampton* and Belfast tugs *Audacious* and *Piper* moved the great new ship away from the wharf slowly, almost reluctantly. While *Canberra* was being nudged astern down to the lighthouse, the huge crowds on the opposite side of the slip started to move with her. First at a mere snail's pace, and then working up to a brisk walking speed, they kept pace with her, some fighting back the tears as they stayed with *Canberra* as far as they could. Once beyond the lighthouse senior Belfast and Trinity House pilot, Arthur Trace, turned her bows towards the Victoria Channel as he took her out to sea on her way to Southampton for drydocking.

Belfast harbour was closed to all other traffic during the tricky manoeuvres *Canberra* had to make. Yet whatever disruption this may have caused to the city's shipping activity, it was nothing to the monumental traffic congestion ashore in Belfast and Holywood. The Sydenham bypass had become a veritable grandstand from which motorists watched the ship's departure.

Northern Ireland's Prime Minister, Lord Brookebrough, Lady Brookebrough and Denis Rebbeck stayed aboard *Canberra* for the day, disembarking by tender at Bangor Bay. Though it was evening as the dignitaries went ashore in County Down, the beaches were packed with people. One woman came forward, tugged at the Prime Minister's sleeve, and said, 'God bless you sorr. Please send us another'.

With a large contingent of Harland & Wolff yardmen still aboard finishing up various tasks of outfitting, *Canberra* was first dry-docked in Southampton's King George V graving dock for a thorough inspection of her hull, whose bottom had not been seen since the day she was launched. That pronounced satisfactory, she proceeded north to run her sea trials off the west coast of Scotland. These operations would put her through her paces and serve to identify any snags that would not become apparent alongside the fitting out wharf. All of the ship's machinery, navigating equipment and other systems were carefully watched and checked throughout the programme. Turning and manoeuvring tests were made and the fin stabilisers were tested. At one point the engines were stopped and final calibration of the magnetic compasses made. Once the builders' and owners' representatives were satisfied with the results of all these tests *Canberra* moved to the mouth of the Clyde to run her speed trials over the measured mile.

It is on the results of this last test that a ship is

finally determined to meet her contract specifications, and the final instalment on the contract price is paid to the builders. If a ship fails to meet her contract speed, she may well be rejected outright, as had been done in a few cases in the early years of steam. Just about any other sort of difficulty can be put right as a part of the ship's acceptance.

*Canberra*'s trials revealed some difficulties of trim, with her stern sitting deeper in the water than expected. Despite the great care taken by everyone concerned with regard to the weight of the machinery and everything else which was supposed to counterbalance its mass forward, she ended up some 500 tons overweight astern. It was only when running trials at sea that the impact of this on her lengthwise balance and handling characteristics could be fully determined. The matter was quite quickly settled between P&O and

C*anberra departing from Belfast on her way to her new home in Southampton.*

*The tourist class children's playroom with its facilities to keep the little ones amused for weeks on end.*

Harland & Wolff. The immediate remedy was to remove some non-essential items astern. Thus a rather heavy wooden suspended canopy ceiling in the Peacock Room was sacrificed, and farther forward the fountains were also taken out of the William Fawcett Room, although the main complaint in this case was that they did not work properly. Applying the old playground seesaw trick, ballast was added in the forward hull compartments to help alleviate the problem by, in effect, pulling the bow down a bit.

While Harland & Wolff had a sound reputation for building 'heavy', *Canberra*'s added depth and less agile handling characteristics now contrasted more sharply with Vickers-Armstrong's typically lighter construction of *Oriana* and her far nimbler manoeuvrability. However, despite whatever feelings of dissatisfaction there were at the time of her trials, and some compromise of her technical performance, she ultimately was to become a very popular and profitable ship. *Canberra* was officially handed over to P&O at Greenock, minus the various bits and pieces taken off to lighten her stern. The public was unaware of any problems as the ship was promoted to the press on her voyage back to Southampton.

The trip back down to Southampton over the Whitsun bank holiday weekend was an opportunity to show the flag, and the ship herself, to the nation, as her course took her close inshore at more than sixty towns, resorts and beauty spots. *Canberra* left the Clyde on Saturday night, passed Douglas on the Isle of Man, and moved along the Welsh and North Devon coasts through Sunday. Early Monday she rounded Land's End and spent the whole day hugging the southern coast of England in brilliant sunshine, all the way across to Southampton. *The Daily Telegraph*'s correspondent Neil Potter told of more that a hundred small boats coming out in the morning from Torquay to welcome *Canberra*. At Exmouth the ship stopped to pose for photographers. In the afternoon thousands on foot thronged the cliff tops all the way from Start Point to Berry Head. That evening *Canberra* tied up at her new terminal in Southampton's Western Docks.

While some 300 Harland & Wolff workers had been setting various technical kinks to rights and putting the finishing touches to cabins, stairway handrails and a host of other details, *Canberra* had also hosted some 600 guests for a pre-maiden voyage of their proud new flagship. Among the VIPs, company and shipping people, travel agents and press was *Punch*'s J B Boothroyd. Although puzzled by the missing canopy ceiling in the Peacock Room and William Fawcett fountain, which had been left behind in Scotland, he penned the sort of characteristically entertaining account of his impression of *Canberra* for which the magazine is so well known.

### The Wind Blows Free
*By J B Boothroyd*

One point that future P&O brochures might make about *Canberra* is that kiddies peering through the periscope of the model spaceship in one of their playrooms, (I can't remember which, but the one with the model spaceship) can see what their parents are up to on the sun-deck above, where the frail blondes and hairy he-men are draped along the terraces of the first class swimming pool. This is all right as long as the parents are together and behaving themselves; but separated and mispaired they could be in for some embarrassing disclosures when their little ones are being tucked down for the night. After a few of these reports have come in, you are going to get a situation where the kids can't get into the spaceship for queues of mothers and fathers waiting to take a reading.

Even a ship as highly-organised socially as the *Canberra* could soon get out of phase with this sort of thing: children excluded from the spaceship spilling over into the teenagers' room...teenagers finding juke-box jiving intolerable with tots tripping them up right and left and transferring their activities to the Peacock Room...where listeners to the permanently piped light music are dislodged into a programme of recorded Beethoven in the Library...until their philistine attitude towards the classics drives the intellectual along into the Cricketer's Bar...there to discuss the Leonora No. 2 so aggressively that the denizens proper, drinking up, bid farewell to Ruskin Spear's life-size portraits of Grace, Bradman, Constantine and Ranjitsinhji and crowd unhappily into the William Fawcett Room, awed a little by the fluorescent fountains, bronzed green leather and mirror-glass murals, but possibly comforted by the dramatic recital of Bingo numbers. It could end with all two thousand two hundred and thirty eight passengers abandoning the other thirteen decks and trying to find asylum on the bridge.

I may say that this situation showed no sign of developing during my three days on board, and this may well have been because

there wasn't a child on the ship from end to end. No one who has never sailed in a childless luxury liner can know what this means. No screams from the paddling pool. No tears at the table. No shouts of 'Mummy, Mummy' outside the ship's shops. I am in no position, of course, to guarantee these conditions on future voyages. Two days from now, when she leaves Southampton for Fremantle, Melbourne, Sydney, Auckland, Honolulu and places of that kind, childish voices will mingle with others to shake the decorative ceilings of these palatial chambers. What I can guarantee is (a) they won't shake anything in the room next door owing to a lot of mysteriously efficient sound-proofing and (b) that any shaking by voices, childish or adult, will be about the only shaking there is, owing to a lot of mysteriously efficient engineering. There are some ships, as none will deny, where a man trying to get his hand to his evening tie sees it leaping in the mirror as if afflicted with Parkinson's Disease. In the *Canberra* he's in for a different kind of alarm, which I saw registered on many an experienced sailing face...that sudden detachment from conversation, the head cocked, the eyes wearing a listening look...then the whisper goes round, pretending a mere curiosity, but expressing a cold unease...'Why have we stopped?' But in the *Canberra* we haven't stopped. A look over the rail shows the sea still going comfortingly past at 27 knots. This is all to do with Mr T W Bunyan BSc, MIMechE and so forth, who got a gold medal out of the Institute of Marine Engineers for a paper entitled 'The Practical Approach to Some Vibration and Machinery Problems in Ships', and under this encouragement went on to put 85,000 shaft horse-power into this ship. I should like to add my endorsement to the Institute's choice of medallist. They

could recognise a practical approach when they saw one all right.

The last thing I want to do is injure the P&O in any way, especially after their recent hospitality, which included three green swizzle sticks they don't know about, but my honest inclination would be to warn future *Canberra* passengers against forking out for a first class passage. To put it rather sweepingly, about all they are going to get for the extra money is relief from the soiled feeling when they come up against a notice saying First Class Only; and surely the truly adult-minded can rise above a little thing like that? During the recent journalists' benefit we were all given the run of the ship; well, within limits, I mean; no one, so far as I know, tried to gatecrash the crew's swimming pool, the stabiliser compartment or the laundry (though the wheelhouse was crowded most of the time, and many of us experienced a sharp drop of confidence when we saw that the man at the helm, with three hundred yards of ship behind him, was steering with a wheel apparently out of a child's motor-car and the bottom half missing at that); but it was only by reference to the plans of the ship, jutting from every pocket, that we could determine whether we were for the moment dinner-jacketed first class or out-at-elbows tourist. No noticeable thinning of carpets. No sudden inequality of table legs. No stark utilitarianisation of fixtures and fittings.

Not even a patronising lowering of standards on the artistic/decorative side. You might think, leaving the first class restaurant with its interestingly shapeless shapes of 'bone, metal, etc., inlaid into Indian laurel' and moving into the second class restaurant, that you would be deprived of modern art. Not a bit of it. There you find cast aluminium screens with multilateral holes knocked in them and filled with green glass (as I recollect). In the first class lounge the central light fitting is a 20-foot square moon landscape in what could well be zinc, with naked bulbs in the valleys. Does this mean that the tourist class equivalent ignores the march of design? Certainly not. Dishes rise from a honeycomb of black flower pots. And the dishes light up at night. So fairly, in fact, have these favours been distributed, that at the time of writing, ten hours after leaving the ship, I can't remember which class enjoys what. I have an *aide memoire*, certainly – a handout entitled 'Some of the Decorative Features in *Canberra*' – but the compiler's language tends to be technical. Where exactly, and indeed what, were the 'two large sculpted fountains continuously pumping effervescent water through asymmetrically placed vertical features'? Exactly which murals were 'painted on to melamine-impregnated Perstorp laminate'? And I seem to have missed completely the Peacock Room's 'floating ceiling, a radial design in painted timber members'.

Ah well. You can't see everything in three days. Passengers making the round trip from next Friday onwards (taking in San Francisco, Los Angeles, and so on, back at Southampton 1 September) will have time to study the whole thing at leisure. I envy them – not least for being able to find from £772 to £1,776 first class return, or from £494 to £628 tourist. I can't quite imagine how this feels. On my trip, admittedly shorter, I was in the humiliating position of being taken for nothing.

*Punch*, 31 May 1961

*The Island Room had a stark modern decorative scheme which was intended to be the background for passengers to provide their own colour and animation on the dance floor.*

# 'SHE'S HERE'

*Canberra*'s commercial career started on Friday 2 June 1961, as she sailed under the command of Captain Geoffrey Wild for a three month voyage to Australia, New Zealand, Hawaii and the Pacific ports of Canada and the United States, and returning by the same route. *Canberra* took her place as the flagship of the combined P&O and Orient Line fleets, then numbering eighteen passenger ships, which together served all continents except South America and Antarctica. On the previous day, while BBC television was filming the departure preparations with Pat Walker and David Hannon, Captain Wild was appointed P&O's commodore. In praise of his futuristic new ship which 'seems to have advanced at least a decade', over *Iberia* and *Arcadia* Wild said:

> Size and speed alone has not made *Canberra* the world's most advanced liner... It was the will of the creators to produce a revolutionary ship with wisdom, taking into consideration the trends and changes within the past twenty-five years to make her a vessel which is different.

A *traditional fireboat welcome from* Abner T Longley *as* Canberra *enters Honolulu Harbour on 12 July 1961.*

*Plotting a course with* Canberra*'s 24in 'bright-display' radar equipment, which was state of the art for its time.*

He was confident of his crew, many of whom had previously served with him in other P&O ships, and of their ability to make some 2,200 passengers feel at ease and at home aboard *Canberra*, as he added, 'The biggest problem we envisage is to keep the intimacy which has been one of the features of P&O ships in the past'.

*Canberra*'s outward voyage was fully booked, her passengers including 750 travelling on 'assisted passages' to new homes and lives in Australia and another 120 emigrating to New Zealand. Along with the Belfast yardmen William Lucas, Billy Cadoo and Francis Bingham and their families, were Mac and Margaret Mchugh and their children, Helen, James and Ruth. Saddened at leaving the sixteenth-century cottage in Somerset which had been their home and at parting with family and friends of a lifetime, they were at the same time excited about

the bright prospects of a new life under Queensland's blue tropical skies. They were absolutely thrilled to have been given passage on *Canberra*'s maiden voyage, and, no doubt like many others, felt in their hearts that they might never again enjoy so memorable a shipboard experience.

In first class was Alice Lovely, a widow in her early sixties who had discovered the pleasures of sea travel in the new life she had made for herself after her husband's untimely death eight years earlier. For Mrs Lovely this was to be the beginning of an affinity with *Canberra* that would last throughout the ship's career, and a special sense of belonging to a large worldwide 'family' which would over the years grow up around the ship, her officers and crew and her many repeat passengers.

The departure from Southampton was postponed by an hour owing to some unexplained engine-room troubles. As *Canberra*'s passengers eagerly waited to get underway, afternoon tea was served. While Mac Mchugh looked after the children in their cabin, Margaret went below to the Atlantic Dining Room. There she talked with another lady at her table who confided feeling that the delay was an ill omen, explaining, 'You do realise that this ship was built in the same dock as the Titanic...and you know what happened to that'. Relieved that her shipmate had not actually seen anything so ominous as seawater pouring into *Canberra*'s lower decks somewhere or another, Mrs Mchugh assured her that she doubted that there would be any icebergs in the Red Sea.

As *Canberra* approached Port Said for the first time on 8 June, she passed P&O's old *Strathaird*, homeward bound on her last voyage from Australia before being delivered to Hong Kong for scrapping. It was one of those poignant moments which occur from time to time in maritime history and which ships' officers and crews hold very dear to their hearts. As the two passed port side to port

side, whistles and sirens were sounded and the flags aboard both ships dipped in salute. *Strathaird*'s master, Captain A E Clay, hailed his counterpart on *Canberra*'s streamlined aluminium bridge with these words:

> You look magnificent, and all in *Strathaird* wish you a happy and successful voyage, and from the old to the new, *Strathaird* bids you farewell.

Recalling, no doubt, his own service in the veteran liner, in which so many of *Canberra*'s company had also served, Wild bade farewell on *Canberra*'s behalf to the ship which thirty years earlier had looked to her own illustrious future as the second of P&O's then modern 'White Sisters':

> You too look magnificent with your paying off pennant flying gaily. You look a gracious and not too elderly lady. All well here.

It was the '*Straths*' which had first replaced on a permanent basis P&O's earlier colour scheme of black hull and stone-coloured upperworks, with the all-white hull and superstructure and buff for funnels and masts used for its passenger ships ever since. *Canberra* was in fact replacing *Strathaird*, the last of the slower liners on the Australian run, and, with *Oriana*, completing the transition to the new faster and extended service.

*Canberra*'s maiden voyage was enthusiastically celebrated at each of the ports she visited, with the magnificent white liner being widely hailed as the 'new look' ship which everyone was sure would appear modern for many years to come and would set a new pattern for future liners of the coming space age. It was then that her passengers and the thousands of others who turned out to see her at Gibraltar, Naples, Port Said and Aden could see and experience why she had been called the ship which shapes the future.

*Aden was an important stop for bunkering on the Australia run, and a popular attraction for passengers too.*

As might well be expected of something as radically new and different as *Canberra*, there were the inevitable technical hitches which threatened to cast shadows of doubt over her debut. During the voyage a leakage in the condenser tubing began to manifest itself, wreaking havoc with the ship's schedule. Seawater, used as a coolant so that the condensers could reclaim boiler feed water from spent steam exiting the turbines, was seeping into the condenser tubing and causing contamination of the feed water supply, with the risk of seriously damaging *Canberra*'s high-powered boilers.

In the Red Sea trouble developed with the port-side condenser, causing a fourteen hour delay at Aden. There, electrical power was lost altogether for a while, leaving *Canberra* without air conditioning in Arabia's searing summer heat. An announcement was made that passengers could, if they wished, take their bedding up on deck for the night. The Mchugh children were already tucked in for the night and the cabin was still cool, so Mac and Margaret decided not to disturb them. Most passengers went ashore the next day for sightseeing in Crater and Sheik Othman or shopping at Steamer Point. Meanwhile, new condenser components flown out from England were fitted and tested as the crew bore the brunt of the discomfort. The long sea-legs of the journey to Colombo and from there to Fremantle were

already planned to be run at near full speed, leaving no margin for *Canberra* to make up the lost time.

At Fremantle, with *Canberra* then thirty-one hours behind schedule, Australians turned out en masse to greet and welcome their new ship. They jammed the shores and the harbour, enthusiastically cheering and blasting their car horns. It seemed that the whole of Western Australia had turned out for the occasion. Two days later, with yet more time lost to the persistent condenser difficulties,

*The Sydney Harbour Bridge forms the backdrop for* Canberra *on an early voyage to Australia.*

and with no help from the prevailing winds, *Canberra* received another tumultuous Australian welcome at Melbourne, where the Lucas, Cadoo and Bingham families headed for their new jobs at the Whyalla shipyard. In Melbourne Dame Pattie Menzies boarded *Canberra* for the privilege of sailing into Sydney in the ship she had launched. She was delighted to see the finished ship, and showed great interest in her operations.

When *Canberra* sailed under the Sydney Harbour Bridge in the brilliant morning sunshine of 28 June, P&O's great white ship of the future brought Australia's largest city to a veritable standstill. The Mchugh family disembarked and said goodbye to the beautiful vessel which had brought them to Australia in such fine style. As

they boarded a train for the overnight journey to Brisbane they could not have known that their voyage had been a good omen for the bright future which lay ahead for them.

Her arrival was the second and final resounding salvo in a P&O publicity campaign orchestrated to promote both *Oriana* and *Canberra* to the Australian travelling public, not only for the services to England and Europe, but also for their new Pacific routes which would take them to North America, the Pacific islands and the Far East. The press build-up to *Oriana*'s arrival in Sydney had been so great that on the day of her arrival, banner headlines in the Sydney newspaper

*Jim Davis, manager of Corporate Affairs at P&O, being greeted by Miss Hawaii during welcoming celebrations aboard* Canberra *in Honolulu.*

*The Sun* had merely to proclaim 'She's Here' and everybody knew exactly who 'She' was. Six months later 'She' would refer to *Canberra*.

*Canberra*'s reception in Sydney was every bit as enthusiastic. It turned out that, apart from the success of her own debut, *Oriana* had provided the build-up to *Canberra*, 'the diminuendo to the *Canberra*'s crescendo', as Sir Colin Anderson had put it during a press conference. Everyone knew that of the two ships she was the one with engines aft which held the promise of the future. While the Sydney Opera House was yet to be planned, Australia's own future appeared to be taking shape in the form of a number of waterfront high-rise buildings under construction near the newly-opened ocean terminal which received *Canberra*'s passengers.

On the day of *Canberra*'s arrival the *Sydney Morning Herald* carried a commentary by Neville Pixley, Chairman of P&O-Orient Lines of Australia, expressing a contemporary view of *Canberra* and of her future outlook in the jet age as it appeared before the divergent, though ultimately complementary, developments of the jumbo jet and the modern cruise ship:

> *Canberra* has rightly been called a floating showcase of beauty and craftsmanship. We are justifiably proud of her – proud not only of her immense size, comfort and revolutionary design, but also of the role she is destined to play in making ocean travel faster and more interesting for her passengers.... Into *Canberra* and *Oriana* went all the fruits of century-old experience in running passenger services. We have been carrying Australians for a long time, and we feel we know their wants and requirements. We are providing even higher standards.... Sometimes we are asked about the future of sea travel in this age of jet aircraft.

*Canberra* and *Oriana* provide one answer. Nothing can match the beauty and romance of a great ship – and we believe there will always be people who like to relax while they speed across the oceans rather then being fired like bullets from one continent to another.

In an entirely separate enterprise, the W D & H O Wills tobacco company were planning the release of a new slim filter-tipped cigarette in Australia under the brand name 'Canberra'. Realising the tremendous marketing potential of being associated with the ultra-modern ship of the same name, the firm arranged for their product's launch to coincide with the liner's maiden voyage. The distinctively packaged smokes in their new-design, slim flip-top packs and larger 200 cigarette cases were sold on board *Canberra*, prior to their official release in Sydney at the time of the ship's arrival there, but the brand ultimately did not become anything like as successful as the ship which shared its name.

On to New Zealand, with *Canberra* by then having lost forty-eight hours in her schedule, it was the mighty hand of Nature, rather than the troublesome condenser tubes, which took a turn at holding up her maiden arrival in Auckland. Fog, 'as thick as a hedge' in Commodore Wild's words, kept the ship at anchor off the Rangitoto Beacon while the pilot boat and another launch loaded with custom and port officials each lost their way looking for the stranded liner. With senior harbour pilot Captain J R Smith finally on *Canberra*'s bridge nearly two hours late at 11:45hrs, it took two

Commodore Wild with a member of the San Francisco port authority during welcoming ceremonies on the maiden voyage.

attempts to finally bring the liner alongside against a fast rip tide at 14:30hrs. Passengers with airline connections missed their planes, while sightseeing arrangements were either cancelled or shortened. Nonetheless, *Canberra* was given a civic reception and was visited by New Zealand's Prime Minister Keith Holyoake, and Britain's Secretary for Commonwealth Relations, Mr Duncan Sandys, before she set off on the transpacific portion of her voyage. After stopping at Honolulu, *Canberra* was most enthusiastically welcomed in North America, where she first called at Vancouver and then San Francisco. As the ship passed beneath the span of Golden Gate Bridge, one of her officers scanned the horizon and exclaimed, 'We're in the wrong century; they're expecting a bloody clipper ship!' What he saw was a scene from the 1850s, as a Union Jack was run up the old semaphore mast on Telegraph Hill. Cannons boomed out a 13-gun salute and a whiskered town crier on horseback led a Wells Fargo stagecoach down from Telegraph Hill proclaiming 'Hear-ye, hear-ye, the *Canberra* is here'. She was welcomed to America in traditional '49er Gold Rush' style. Through a live, closed-circuit television link-up a broadcast of *Canberra*'s arrival, hosted by Basil Rathbone, was made to gatherings of media, travel and tourist people in New York, Chicago and Toronto. Sir Donald Anderson and Captain Wild were also invited to the office of the Mayor of San Francisco where they were presented with keys to the city.

When *Canberra* arrived at Long Beach, outside Los Angeles, southern California welcomed her with similar enthusiasm. There a contingent of US Marines greeted her with a 50-gun salute, and Australian Beauty Queen, Rosemary Fenton, led a kangaroo along the pier as *Canberra* docked, symbolising the ship's naming in honour of the Australian capital city.

Despite her engine troubles, fog and a few

*The Mayor of San Francisco presents the key to the City to Commodore Wild and Sir Donald Anderson.*

other minor setbacks, *Canberra* had made a magnificent debut. Sir Donald, who was aboard for parts of the outward journey said of the technical problems that they were no more than a 'blistered heel on the foot of a great athlete.' He had observed every aspect of his new ship's operation and had duly noted various points to be looked into. Before going on by air from Sydney to rejoin *Canberra* in Honolulu he sent a long litany of observations and suggestions back to London.

He was not happy with the organisation of the first class shop. The passengers' launderettes, a

new feature of *Canberra*, appeared to need some sort of supervision to curtail wasteful use of the washing machines and tumble dryers. The libraries needed to be better organised to prevent passengers from re-shelving books in the wrong places. Night bolts needed to be fitted on cabin doors to prevent stewards from entering while passengers were dressing or undressing, as the soundproofing was so effective it even prevented them from hearing passengers' answers of 'come in' or 'stay out' when they knocked. The barriers between first and tourist classes were insufficient, with the doors between the two halves of the ship constantly being left open. Were too many towels and table napkins being used? Would it be possible to charge for some extras such as meals served in cabins and catering of private cocktail parties?

Recommendations were made that the table cloths in the first class dining room should be cut so that they could be placed around the table

lamps without the fixtures themselves having to be dismantled. Finally, he felt that of all *Canberra*'s public rooms only the Stadium, an indoor/outdoor sports deck area behind the Crow's Nest observation, had been a flop, largely because of difficulties in keeping its retractable roof closed in high winds. After returning home, *Canberra* would be in Southampton for two weeks, when all these things could be looked at in detail.

The trip home itself was quite uneventful, with the condenser problem seemingly having been put right for the time being at least. After departing from Naples, *Canberra* encountered the Italian liner *Leonardo da Vinci* outward bound for New York. A near contemporary of the new-look P&O flagship, *Leonardo da Vinci*, with her single funnel amidships and superb balance of line and form, showed the alternative approach of rendering timeless classicism into a modern expression of beauty.

*In Long Beach, California,* Canberra *is appropriately greeted by a kangaroo led by Australian beauty queen Rosemary Fenton.*

# PASSAGES

In her early years, *Canberra*'s career still belonged very much to the liner era, when the majority of people on board would be making passages to far-away destinations rather than returning to their embarkation point as cruise passengers do. The feeling of being aboard ships then, when there was a far greater sense of purpose, or even destiny, in what everybody was doing, was quite different from the modern cruising experience.

Sir Hugh Casson expressed the feeling of this classic era of ocean travel in the introduction to a paper he wrote some years later for a special edition of *The Architectural Review*, commemorating Britain's next great shipbuilding triumph, *Queen Elizabeth 2*. The new Cunard flagship had yet to sail on her maiden voyage, and Sir Hugh's reflections no doubt recalled his involvement with, and very special affinity for, *Canberra*.

*Canberra lit by the late afternoon sun on the Mediterranean waters she has sailed in both line service and her later cruising career.*

### A Ship is an Island
*by Sir Hugh Casson*

Inhabited yet mysteriously unexplored, self-centred, secretive, wonderful, unique. Silhouetted against a sunset horizon or towering white-topped above a quayside, ablaze with lights or gay with flags, it seems cut off in time as well as space – a presence whose scale is impossible to grasp, and whose indifference to admiration is as maddening as a cat's. Arrivals and departures are movements of effortless separation and rejoining. There is none of the heart-in-mouth drama of take-off and touch-down. Movements are almost imperceptible, voices pitched low. The strip of water widens or narrows, a hawser splashes, a tiny figure signals from aloft and it is done. A lifeline has been cut, the real world drops away as suddenly as a garment, its most commonplace features to be greeted on the day of landfall with astonishment. . . 'Look, dear, there's a bus!' On board the pages of the traveller's diary lie white and empty like sheets turned down upon an expectant bed. Despite every manner of ingenious device, communication with the shore seems pointless and absurd. The ship's newspaper – even the magically reproduced miniaturised facsimile of a London edition – for all its relevance might be reporting items from the Moon. Mitty-like dreams of storm and conquest and adventure sink into a gorgeous routine of dozing, eating, sleeping, reading and gossip. Spare time, 'that blessed void' lies waiting to be filled in a private stylish cocoon of polished corridors, soft lights, solicitous attendants and regular nourishment.

To be for a time a voluntary member of this captive community, a conscripted voluptuary as it were, is a unique experience taken too often with too little wonder at those human skills that have devised for us this strange environment. Admittedly in these days of technical fireworks we are difficult to surprise. To move at 600mph, and 30,000ft while sipping a Martini and watching a movie has become, we know, a commonplace experience.

But at sea, where the elements in all their changing moods can be seen, smelled and even felt at close quarters, there is less excuse for such a detached and blasé view. It is not so very long ago, after all, that a sea voyage was as irregular, unpredictable, and certainly quite as uncomfortable, as a family picnic. It began when everybody was ready and finished as the luck of the weather might decide. But the arrival of steam and steel, the establishment of regular routes and fixed timetables ... transformed the picture, until today we take a ship's punctuality for granted. We grumble without shame at an hour's delay in a week's voyage and, when they fail us, it is not the failure of some impersonal mechanism, but of a faithless mistress. This love-hate relationship between the traveller and his means of transport is centuries old and worldwide and notably capricious in effect. Motor cars, once as cherished, groomed and regularly exercised as horses, are now as anonymous as milk bottles. Trains are still admired from the platform but treated by the voyager, once onboard as shabbily as litter-bins. Aircraft have kept their power to awe and even to alarm but seldom to inspire love. Hovercraft with their capricious skirts arouse curiosity but little else. Ships alone invite and receive an affection that is almost personal in its intensity.

*The Architectural Review*, June 1969

*Christmas comes to* Canberra *during an outward Australian passage in the early years.*

*Canberra*'s long route, taking her two-thirds of the way around the globe, spanned the northern and southern hemispheres, where the high- and off-seasons were at different times of the year. Voyages starting during the British high-season months of June, July and August would bring passengers to Australia in the off-season there, with the opportunity of providing winter voyages from Sydney and Auckland to the Pacific and North America. Low-season pre-Christmas sailings from Southampton would bring *Canberra* from Britain's winter cold and darkness into the Australian summer and holiday season, offering opportunities for holiday voyages in the Pacific while it would still be too early for Australians to want to travel to Europe. Getting on towards springtime in Japan, the ship could return to Southampton via the Far East, taking in Yokohama, Hong Kong and Singapore on the way home. This scheme left enough latitude for a number of short cruises to be tried while filling in gaps in the schedule as the seasons changed around the globe.

At the time of *Canberra*'s debut, air travel was still somewhat élitist and relatively expensive, with a one-way ticket from London to Sydney costing £248 for a sleepless odyssey of thirty-five hours.

*Geishas greet the great liner on her first arrival at Yokohama in 1961.*

*Canberra*'s fares for a twenty-six-day passage to Sydney ran from £150 for basic shared accommodation to £550 for a single cabin with its own en-suite bathroom. Lower fares were offered for off-season sailings, while an even less expensive 'Boomerang' ticket could be bought for round-trip travel for as little as £290 for first class cabins.

However, the many thousands of people who emigrated to Australia on assisted passages paid only £10 per adult against the cost of what amounted to a bulk chartering of tourist class accommodation by the Australian government. Their children, baggage and personal belongings were carried at no charge. In those days, before the advent of large wide-bodied airliners, ships offered the most economical way of transporting such large numbers of people taking all their personal belongings with them.

Australia House in effect had first priority on all of the tourist class accommodation. Their passengers were, for administrative purposes at least, divided into three categories: professional, such as doctors and engineers; skilled workers, including teachers, machinists and various other specialist tradespeople; and the large numbers of ordinary workers and labourers Australia so needed in those years. P&O's policy was that these people were all nonetheless passengers, and that they were to be treated with the same respect and courtesy as any passenger paying a full fare. There was to be no distinction made on board which would set those on assisted passages apart from anyone else in tourist class.

These were mostly young families, and there were inevitably large numbers of children. P&O then organised educational programmes on all their ships for the school-aged youngsters, which were run by teachers among the assisted-passage passengers who could be identified from the lists provided by Australia House. At a reception given for them at the beginning of the voyage, they would be asked to participate on a voluntary basis. The next day, parents would sign their children up for the informal curriculum and the programme would get under way the following morning. On the days spent at sea, a recording of *The Syncopated Clock* would be played over the broadcast system, summoning the children to their shipboard classes after breakfast. The programme was kept fairly light, with not too much long multiplication, fractions and spelling, and was made enjoyable with tours of the bridge, galley and engine room, and with ice cream being served up at breaktimes.

In her memoirs, Margaret Mchugh recalled the 'quaint' berthing arrangements which were made for the four families which shared their block of cabins surrounding one of the short sideways passages. One cabin was assigned to the mother and children of each family, while the four husbands were berthed together in a fifth room. Once everyone had settled in, she recalled, they redistributed themselves to suit each family's own conveniences, as no doubt did most others who had been likewise split up.

While assisted passages were then a substantial part of P&O's bread-and-butter trade, both *Canberra* and *Oriana* were also highly prestigious ships which carried their share of the famous and prominent people of their early days. As one of the ship's later captains, Jock Lefevre, recalled, '*Canberra* engaged the last of the Raj'. Among these were Sir Donald and Lady Bradman, who sailed on *Canberra* with their son, John. The England and Australian cricket Test teams were regular passengers in those days, as were the newspaper proprietor Lord Kemsley and Lady Kemsley. Former Labour minister Lord George Brown, too, later tried one of *Canberra*'s early Caribbean Cruises. The film star Cary Grant also took a liking to the great white British ship, travelling aboard her a number of times over the years

In both first and tourist classes, *Canberra,* with her wide range of public rooms, three pools and ample deck space, offered a lifestyle which was up-to-date for the times, yet still far from the sophistication of today's cruise experiences. Most people were then travelling from one place to another, which was in itself a stimulant for social contact

*The 1962-3 Australian Test Team aboard* Canberra *with Commodore Geoffrey Wild.*

and interaction. It was an era of elegance, when people in both classes not only dressed in their finest for dinner, but men also appeared in collar and tie and the ladies in dresses and high-heeled shoes for afternoon tea in the lounge. Although the mode of dress has since become far more casual, evening dress standards aboard *Canberra* have remained fairly formal compared with many other cruise ships.

There was not the professional entertainment then that ships provide today, although there were orchestras for evening dancing in both classes. Daytime activities centred around the pools and deck activities, which included organised tournaments of one kind or another and the spontaneous shipboard pastimes of promenading or merely attending whatever else was happening on deck from the vantage point and socialising position of a deck chair. Bingo, or Housie Housie as it was then more widely known aboard ship, was as popular as it has ever been. During the 1962 season Staff Captain Walter Vickers organised afternoon cha-cha instruction in the hopes that the dance floors would not empty so quickly during the evening hours whenever the band struck up a number with a latin beat.

The baby-boom era was coming of age, with *Canberra*'s many teenage passengers being given their own space, the Pop-Inn. This turned out to be one of the busiest places in the ship. There, a shiny, brightly-illuminated juke box was kept stocked with all the latest hit records, including Chubby Checker, Frank Sinatra, Petula Clark and, later on, the Beatles and The Rolling Stones, along with Australia's own Bee Gees and Seekers. The twist was one of the first teenage dance crazes to hit *Canberra* in 1962. The only complaint that the 'teenie boppers' had about this, their very own space, was that the older folks would pour in to try the newest dance steps after their Bingo sessions had ended in the William Fawcett Room next door.

*A*fternoon tea was an important part of the day in the late sixties aboard both Canberra *and* Oriana.

Directly across from the Pop Inn, on *Canberra*'s port side, the Cricketer's Tavern became equally successful as one of the most remarkable manifestations of the British or Australian pub ever to go to sea. The celebration of cricket, loved as the game is in these two lands, has been a focal point of social activity since long before the present trend for sports bars was ever thought about. While world-renowned cricketers and even one American baseball player contributed autographed items to the room's collection of mementoes, the teenagers were not discouraged from adding their initials to the Pop Inn's graffiti-style poker-work wall, which was created by the then little-known artist David Hockney, before it was removed in an an early refit. The elegantly dark and intimate Century Bar had the atmosphere of a sophisticated club or posh hotel, more in keeping with the designers' perception of first class taste. However, if the truth be known, there was probably far more interloping of first class passengers to the Cricketer's and the Pop Inn in those days than P&O ever knew about.

There was no casino, nor one-armed bandits and fruit machines then. *Canberra* offered shipboard horse racing, where bets would be made on wooden horses moved either by the roll of a dice or hand-cranked by enthusiastic passenger 'jockeys', and there was the daily 'tote' on the ship's progress from noon of one day to the next. Both were eagerly patronised, and they served the purpose of raising funds for seamen's charities. The closest thing to formal entertainment were the Mad Hatter's Ball, which had become the modern substitute for the elaborate fancy dress balls held on liners the world over during the 1930s, and the inevitable concerts put on by passengers and members of the crew themselves for their shipmates. By 23:00hrs, midnight at the very latest, the band had finished playing, the bars were closed and the ship was quiet until the crew emerged in the early hours to clean the public rooms and decks, long before the first risers would appear at daybreak for a dawn stroll around the decks or dip in the pool at sunrise.

For those who missed their 'telly', *Canberra* offered a fairly elaborate closed-circuit broadcasting system for its day, with television sets in a number of the public rooms. The most expensive cabins and suites were also wired for television when the ship was built, although the system was never extended, and received colour televisions in the late 1980s. In the opinion of Commodore John Wacher, who served as *Canberra*'s Staff Captain early in her career before later commanding her, the television system would have better served the needs of the crew in alleviating boredom in their spare time during long turns of duty aboard the ship. For passengers the cinema was a far greater attraction, equipped as it was to show the latest widescreen CinemaScope films with stereophonic sound.

During those years, *Canberra* and *Oriana* each developed their own characters and loyal follow-

*'With 4 legs' as the David Hockney graphic reads; Sir Donald Anderson's daughters ready to dance the evening away in the teenager's Pop Inn during the maiden voyage.*

ings which they kept through the inevitable later changeover to cruising. While both ships were of similar size, speed and capacity, designed to do the same thing, they turned out to be remarkably different, both in their appearances and in their characters. Rather then being near identical twins as were Moore McCormack's *Argentina* and *Brasil*, broadly similar sisters as were Cunard's *Queen Mary* and *Queen Elizabeth*, *Canberra* and *Oriana* were distinguished fleetmates, each with an identity entirely its own.

So far as outward appearance was concerned, *Oriana* was arguably the more controversial of the two ships. Her design represented an approach which gave the functional efficiency of the ship a higher priority over popularising the ocean-going hotel and resort factors, which had prescribed many of *Canberra*'s design features. *Oriana*'s plan and profile had more to do with the optimum placement of machinery, location of mooring decks for maximum purchase on the lines and reduced superstructure height towards the bow and stern to lessen wind resistance and make the ship easier to turn.

While both were modern ships the impression which they conveyed was of *Oriana* being considered 'old guard' against *Canberra*'s more avant-garde air. This took in the interior design, which in *Oriana*'s case reflected a sense of understated modern elegance introduced with *Orion* in the 1930s, while *Canberra* was considered to be ultra-modern, and a complete break with anything P&O had ever done before. While *Oriana*'s onboard style was predictable, *Canberra*'s wide-spread use of fibreglass, plastics and other new materials, which seemed to belong more to the realm of aircraft outfitting, didn't necessarily please everyone who first saw the ship.

*Canberra*'s layout, with her open under-the-lifeboats promenade deck completely surrounding

*The extremely modern cinema offered another diversion for those long days at sea.*

the public rooms, won immediate favour and has remained a much-appreciated feature of the ship. *Oriana*'s plan, with the public rooms concentrated on the upper decks above her nested boats, and with fully-glassed-in promenades partially surrounding her suite of lounges, came in for some criticism. Passengers at first complained about the ship being too closed in and about the difficulty in getting to anywhere out in the open. The boat deck, which in *Oriana*'s case did not go all the way around the ship, was two flights below the first class lounges, outside the B-deck cabins. Many of the upper decks were also enclosed by full-height glass windscreens. While *Canberra*'s upper decks likewise needed protection from the winds which would swirl around her upperworks at speed, a thoughtful refinement of her design was that the glass windbreaks were set in from the deck edge, leaving a narrow railed-in outer promenade for those who wanted to be at one with the elements.

Beyond these fundamental differences of design approach and layout, *Oriana* possessed a unique, classic tropical liner quality about her.

There were those little things which one would discover during the voyage such as the spiral staircases which joined her boat deck (B deck) with the enclosed promenades two decks higher up. These were intended for crew use only, but would inevitably be discovered by curious passengers. Also to be 'found' was the stairway behind the ballroom stage on Veranda Deck descending to the portside Silver Grill on A deck below, inboard of the lifeboats; its location, too, among the first class cabins had to be discovered.

There were other areas such as the open Junior's Deck, forward of the Princess Room, surrounding Hatch No.3, and the Stadium Deck above, which offered upwards vistas over parts of the superstructure, bridge, deck cranes and other working parts of the ship. These things were strongly reminiscent of Orient Line's earlier ships and the unique experience of travelling aboard them.

*Canberra* was very different in this regard, more rational and modern but, in so being, lacking the same ability to convey that certain sense of wonder about being at sea. Her superstructure, uninterrupted by the all-the-way-aft machinery and funnels and the side-loading lateral cargo transporters of the centremost hatches, provided less insight to her structure and workings while aboard. What the passenger on deck was treated to instead was the clean, slender form of her tall twin tanker-style stacks and the gently curvilinear lines of her bridge housing which dissolved into the tall aluminium mast surmounting it. These things seemed to say more to passengers about the lifestyle to be enjoyed on board than about the life of the ship as a working organism herself.

*Oriana* was the lighter and faster ship. Those who have piloted both will unanimously agree that *Oriana* was as light as a feather to handle, while *Canberra* had a much heavier and even

sluggish feel about her. Commodore John Wacher was always especially fond of *Oriana* and loved the way she handled. On the other hand, Commodore Wild always had a great affinity for *Canberra*, though conceding that 'she didn't turn corners too well'. Harbour pilots always had to be warned to call their turns earlier than usual aboard *Canberra*, and it is thanks to the readily available full reverse power of her turbo electric machinery that the possibilities of an occasional collision or grounding in such circumstances have been averted. Ian Gibb, who was *Canberra*'s master before taking command of the new *Oriana* and attaining the post of Commodore, fondly recalls her being 'a beast to handle. You had to be on your toes taking the Brambles and Calshot turns coming into Southampton at around 05:30hrs in the morning, often in fog, at the end of a voyage'.

*Canberra* has remained in active service the longer of the two ships, with *Oriana* being sold and taking up a static role similar to that of *Queen Mary*, first in Japan and later moving to China. This has been a direct result of *Canberra*'s considerably heavier construction, which has better stood up to the rigours of service on the high seas. *Oriana*, nonetheless, led a relatively charmed and delightfully quiet and uneventful life, while it was *Canberra* that continued to suffer from sporadic technical problems and had to endure the wear and tear of doing 'national service' as a troop carrier, hospital and prison ship.

OVERLEAF
*These Laurence Dunn and Edward Beckett cutaways highlight the differences of layout which in part produced the diverse characters of* Canberra *and* Oriana.

CANBERRA

LAURENCE DUNN

## CUT-AWAY DRAWING OF 'ORIANA'

### BY EDWARD BECKETT

1 Tourist Class Stern
   Gallery Bar
2 Tourist Class Library
3 Tourist Class Juniors Club
4 Tourist Class Lower
   Swimming Pool
5 Tourist Class Verandah Pool
6 Tourist Class Cabins
7 Tourist Class Stadium Deck

8 Tourist Class
   Entrance Hall
9 Cinema
10 First Class Tennis Deck
11 First Class Ballroom
12 First Class Tavern
13 First Class Swimming Pool
14 Tourist Class Restaurant
15 First Class Cabins

16 First Class Stadium
17 First Class Library
18 First Class Restaurant
19 First Class Stadium Room
20 First Class Juniors Club
21 Crew Cabins
22 Crew Swimming Pool
23 Crew Recreation Room

ORIANA
LONDON

# CUT-AWAY DRAWING OF 'CANBERRA'

### BY LAURENCE DUNN, ASSOC.R.I.N.A.

1 Games Arena
2 Observation Lounge
3 The Abolido Club
4 First Class Swimming Pool
5 Glazed Wind Screens
6 First Class Court Cabins
7 First Class Cabins on 'B' Deck
8 Tourist Class Cabins on 'A' Deck
9 Tourist Class Lounge (The Windsor Room)

10 Tourist Class Reading Room
11 Hospital Area
12 Tourist Class Dining-Room
13 First Class Verandah Suites
14 First Class Court Cabins
15 First Class Dining-Room (Restaurant)
16 First Class Galley
17 Cargo Transporters
18 Light and Air Hatch over Crew Swimming Pool

19 Opening for Transverse Propulsion Unit
20 Fresh-water Tank
21 No. 1. Hold and 'Tween Deck
22 No. 2. Hold and 'Tween Decks
23 No. 3. Hold and 'Tween Deck
24 Stabiliser Fins
25 Engine Room
26 Propulsion Motor
27 Boiler Room
28 Open 'A' Bracket supporting Propeller Shaft

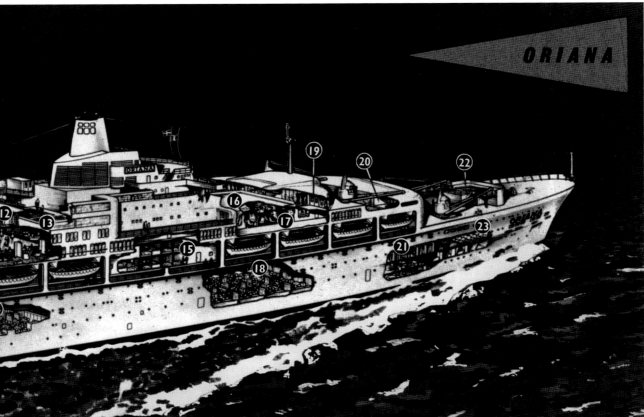

ORIANA

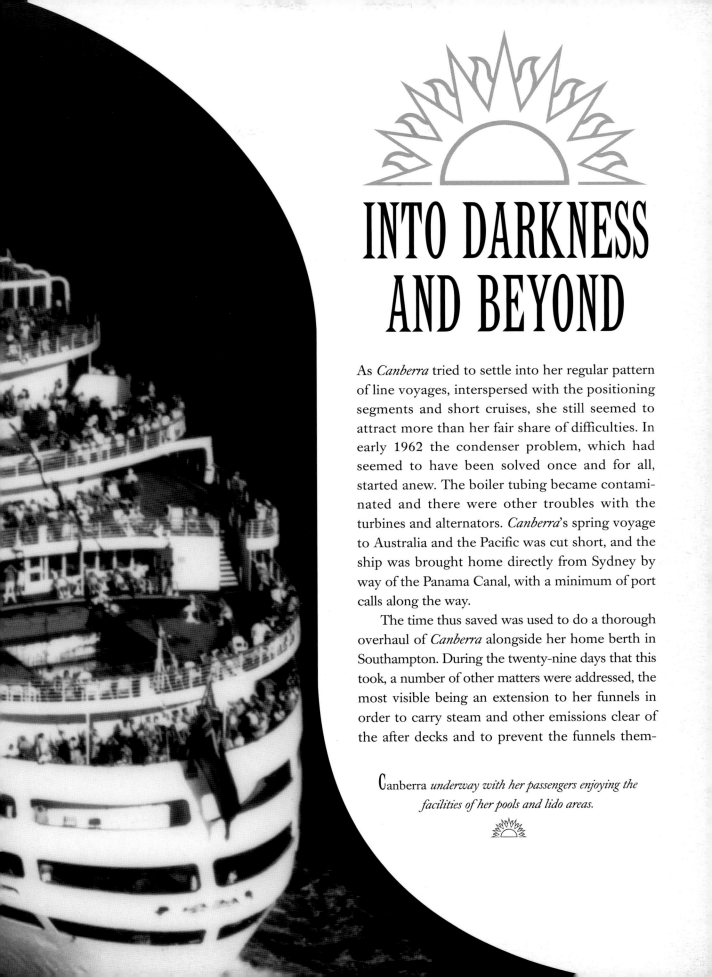

# INTO DARKNESS AND BEYOND

As *Canberra* tried to settle into her regular pattern of line voyages, interspersed with the positioning segments and short cruises, she still seemed to attract more than her fair share of difficulties. In early 1962 the condenser problem, which had seemed to have been solved once and for all, started anew. The boiler tubing became contaminated and there were other troubles with the turbines and alternators. *Canberra*'s spring voyage to Australia and the Pacific was cut short, and the ship was brought home directly from Sydney by way of the Panama Canal, with a minimum of port calls along the way.

The time thus saved was used to do a thorough overhaul of *Canberra* alongside her home berth in Southampton. During the twenty-nine days that this took, a number of other matters were addressed, the most visible being an extension to her funnels in order to carry steam and other emissions clear of the after decks and to prevent the funnels them-

Canberra *underway with her passengers enjoying the facilities of her pools and lido areas.*

Canberra, *with full regalia, entering New York Harbour at the end of her first voyage to 'The Big Apple' in 1962.*

selves from becoming soiled. Also, the troublesome retractable roof over the Stadium Deck was permanently closed in, turning the area into a permanent indoor space which, over the years, has become *Canberra*'s theatre for live entertainment.

It was important for *Canberra* to be in good shape for two back-to-back North Atlantic crossings to New York which had been announced in October 1961. Apart from 'showing the flag' on the eastern seaboard of the United States, this would also serve to test the possibility of a collaborative worldwide operation between P&O and Cunard. This had been discussed between the two Lines as far back as 1959, when Cunard were looking at the contingencies of replacing *Queen Mary* and *Queen Elizabeth*. The basic idea was that *Canberra* and *Oriana* could augment Cunard's summertime North Atlantic capacity during the Australian off-season. For their part, Cunard would provide an

express Atlantic liner, which would offer the type of flexibility that C M Squarey had observed among *Oriana*, *Windsor Castle* and *Leonardo da Vinci*, making that ship suitable for alternative Australian and Pacific services in their high season.

The overall scheme also took in P&O's auxiliary Pacific triangle services being operated by their 28,000-ton ships, combining these with Cunard's intermediate UK/Canadian operation. As Cunard's plans for *Queen Elizabeth 2* subsequently took shape, none of this materialised. After the old *Queens* had been duly disposed of and the *United States* was withdrawn, *QE2* ultimately ended up running in tandem with *France* for the first few years of her career.

*Canberra*'s Southampton to New York crossing of 1962, which was the first commercial P&O voyage on this, Cunard's flagship route, was an immense success. Cunard had chartered P&O's

*Stratheden* to make four voyages to New York in 1950, but P&O themselves had never before attempted the same route. *Canberra* had 1,700 passengers aboard, many of whom made the round trip as a cruise. She was given the traditional New York fireboat welcome, which only a few months earlier had also been accorded to *France*. During the seventy-six hours *Canberra* spent in New York, she was received by the Americans with much the same enthusiasm they had shown on her West Coast maiden calls the previous year. The United States Travel Service took the opportunity to promote British tourism to the USA. The nationwide morning television programme, *The Today Show* was broadcast directly from *Canberra*, showing the new and very 'with it' British liner to an estimated twelve million viewers. It is believed that even President Kennedy saw the broadcast.

The crossing was repeated the following year

*The main engine-room console which had to be wired back on-line after the fire.*

with a single New York round trip made from 24 August to 8 September. This time, while outbound, *Canberra* got a real taste of the North Atlantic, encountering Hurricane Beulah. On the afternoon of 28 August, between 14:00 and 16:00hrs she hove to in 60-knot Force-11 winds to avoid sailing into the eye of the storm. *Canberra* pitched and rolled in 'confused' seas and a heavy swell. On the following day, while steaming at full speed to make up the lost time, she passed three US naval ships engaged in salvage work above the nuclear submarine *Thresher* which had recently sunk in the vicinity. The voyage was otherwise pleasant, with the ship arriving in New York at noon on 30 August and sailing at 13:00hrs on 2 September. On the way home *Canberra* passed and exchanged greetings with *France*, which was inbound to New York. A third trip was made in 1964 to coincide with the World's Fair held in New York that year.

In the meantime, while *Canberra* was outbound on a regular voyage to Australia in early 1963, she suffered what was to be one of the worst mishaps of her long career. At 04:00hrs on Thursday 4 January, while on her way from Naples to Port

Said at 25.5 knots, fire broke out in her engine room. This was caused when a fairly junior electrical engineer tried to correct a situation where one of the generators, which was not running at the time, had started 'motoring'. In a reversal of the normal way things work, current was feeding back to the idle generator from the ship's main electrical switchboard, causing it to function uselessly as a motor spinning the turbine which would normally be driving it to generate power.

This was in fact quite harmless, but the engineer was troubled by the notion that things were not right. He tried to trip the circuit breakers which would have disconnected the flow of power to the generator, but found that the release mechanism would not allow him to break the connection. He made the near-fatal mistake of reaching in behind the panel and releasing the breaker mechanism with his hand. A blinding electric arc, as thick as a tree trunk, virtually melted-down the starboard side of the switchboard, destroying much of the key distribution cabling and starting a serious fire in the generator room which left the turbo-electric *Canberra* dead in the sea. For reasons which nobody could explain, that lethal arc had merely flung the hapless engineer bodily across the engine room to miraculous safety, apart from the inevitable bruises.

*Canberra*'s passengers were mustered to their emergency stations in the Promenade Deck public rooms, while the crew extinguished the blaze. At dawn P&O's homeward-bound *Stratheden* arrived on the scene and stood by the paralysed ship in readiness to take her in tow. In the meantime she kept *Canberra*'s 2,238 passengers and 960 crew supplied with fresh bread, milk, fruit juice and other stores while they waited without light and power. *Canberra*'s crew were praised for their care of the passengers, and in particular for their thoughtfulness in keeping the passengers fully informed on their progress in restoring essential services. Many found this alone to be a source of great comfort and consolation.

Through great resourcefulness and brutally hard work under difficult and dangerous conditions, *Canberra*'s engineers succeeded in restoring emergency power and rigging temporary connections so that one of the main drive motors could be started during that evening. First at a mere 4 knots and then increasing to a steady pace of 10 knots during the night, *Canberra* steamed to the Grand Harbour in Malta, arriving early on Friday morning, 5 January.

There was no question of *Canberra* continuing her voyage, leaving P&O with the colossal challenge of making other arrangements for her huge number of passengers. Ford Geddes, then a director of P&O, arrived in Malta to inspect the damage

*Of course the nation's cartoonists could not miss poking a little good-natured fun at* Canberra's *plight.*

INTO DARKNESS AND BEYOND

*R*esting *quietly at anchor off Malta,* Canberra*'s modern lines contrast with the classical architecture ashore.*

to *Canberra* and to coordinate her evacuation. In London Freddy Laker, who had come up in the airline industry through Silver City, a subsidiary of Britavia which was seventy per cent owned by P&O in the 1950s, was called in to manage an airlift. He set to work immediately, spending the entire weekend at P&O's headquarters in Leadenhall Street in the City of London's Square Mile. Seated at the conference table in the board room with a battery of telephones around him, he swiftly chartered the many aircraft needed to get the stricken ship's passengers on their way to their various destinations.

In that era before today's jumbo jets, and when the Boeing 707s and Douglas DC-8s were still very new, much of the load was split up among numerous Viscounts, Vanguards and Britannias, most of which carried fewer than a hundred passengers. The first sixty-five passengers to return to Britain boarded a British United Airways Viscount bound for Heathrow the following day. Australian authorities arranged flights for the passengers on assisted passages. Those on the round-trip voyage were taken to Naples on chartered ferries, from where they were flown home on scheduled commercial flights. Known as the Malta Airlift, the entire operation took a week to complete, straining Valetta's airport facilities to the limit, with their runways only just able to accommodate the 707s and DC-8s. Laker's greatest skill in this operation was in finding the numbers of planes needed at such short notice and in managing to charter them at reasonable prices.

Some may have looked upon the airlift and the time it took as boding well for the future of sea travel, at least for the time being. The Malta Airlift showed up the still limited capacities of the airlines and of the ground facilities available to them in many places. However, those who were closer to the research and development side of the aircraft industry could already foresee the day when much larger aircraft would be able to compete head on with ships like *Canberra*. Despite the time taken for the airlift, there were many who nonetheless arrived at their destinations two weeks earlier than scheduled and who had to be put up in hotels as they had nowhere else to go until their originally planned arrival dates. Many took the view that their steamship fares had entitled them to three weeks bed and board, which meant that P&O should still look after them for the whole time frame of the passage.

The Rotterdam Lloyd liner *Willem Ruys*, which was also bound for Australia, on a round-the-world voyage, was able to accommodate about 100 of *Canberra's* passengers. The British India cargo ship *Woodara* was dispatched to Malta to take the baggage and cars which were in *Canberra's* holds. Tons of frozen and refrigerated stores, which had started to thaw and spoil during the blackout had to be off-loaded and burned ashore.

Meanwhile, generators were brought alongside *Canberra* to restore power to as many of her cabins and services as possible, enabling her passengers to stay aboard until the last flights departed on 14 January. By that time work had been done onboard which would enable *Canberra* to return to Harland & Wolff under her own steam for complete repairs. She arrived there on 17 March 1963, still with forty-eight passengers aboard who had refused to leave the ship under any circumstances. At a press conference held in *Canberra's* cinema the day she arrived in Belfast, Jim Davis, manager of corporate affairs for P&O, was asked by one reporter why the ship had been brought all the way back to her builders. Sounding rather like a parent discussing the schooling of his children, he answered 'we had to bring her to Belfast because we couldn't get her into Rugby'. This took a lot of pressure off everyone, though reporters continued to hound P&O people for the identity of the

*Daily Express, 8 January, 1963*

"I'm afraid we don't supply a do-it-yourself-get-you-home-aircraft with this one, Sir. Only with the larger models."

*The cartoonists were never unkind to* Canberra: *Giles even sent a copy of this cartoon to P&O on which he touchingly wrote 'With deepest sympathy'.*

engineer who had made the ghastly mistake which caused the fire. His identity was carefully protected, and he had already been spirited away from the ship for his own security. He was never relieved of his post by P&O, though, of his own choice, he never returned to *Canberra*.

*Canberra* was back in service in May. For the following few years her life was quiet and uneventful. One upset was loss of a six-week chunk of the British high-season cruise period in the summer of 1966 during the seamen's strike of that year. During the mid 1960s the remaining pre-Second World War ships, P&O's *Strathmore* and *Stratheden*, along with Orient Line's *Orion*, were withdrawn from service and sold for scrap. At the end of September 1966 the Orient Line's houseflag was

lowered for the last time, ending the history of a great British shipping enterprise, as P&O-Orient Line became once again P&O.

On her June 1967 voyage to Australia *Canberra* came uncomfortably close to being caught in the Suez Canal during the Arab-Israeli war. As the ship approached Port Said, where a midday arrival was planned, Staff Captain Jock Lefevre was making a routine crew accommodation inspection. In one of the rooms he looked into a radio had been left on and, by a lucky coincidence, he heard on the BBC World Service news that Israeli forces had started bombing Port Said. He went immediately to the bridge, where he told the captain that he thought the ship should be turned around immediately. While the two men were discussing the situation a message was received from P&O in London, instructing *Canberra* to return immediately to Gibraltar. There passengers not going all the way to Australia and beyond were either flown on to their destinations or back to England.

*Canberra* then proceeded on her way, reaching Fremantle by way of Cape Town only four days behind schedule. The added costs of the voyage were substantially offset by not having to pay the Suez Canal fees, which had risen sharply since Egypt had taken control of the canal after the 1950s Suez crisis. Had the voyage been planned from the outset to go directly around the Cape of Good Hope without meandering into the Mediterranean almost as far as Port Said, *Canberra* could well have kept to her originally-scheduled calls in Australia. For eight more years she had to travel either by the Cape or Panama. Had she joined a Canal convoy earlier that day in 1967, she could well have been marooned, as a number of other unlucky ships were, for the whole period.

During the last years of the decade onerous signs of doom for the futures of *Canberra* and *Oriana* were quite literally starting to appear in the air. As early as 1962 American plane-makers were thinking about 'growth versions' of early military jet tankers and transports. By 1965 the Boeing Aircraft Corporation dared to think beyond a civilian 'air-bus' adaptation of the military C-5A transport in terms of something far more prestigious, namely their 747 jumbo jet. Five years later the aircraft was in commercial service with the capacity to carry *Canberra*'s entire passenger load from London to Sydney in only six plane loads. BOAC and Qantas were among the first international carriers to order the jumbo. The greater mobility which post-Second World War life had accorded to the masses was to become universal and all-pervasive, ultimately putting international and intercontinental travel within the reach of just about everyone.

At the same time Australia's needs were changing and assisted passages were only now available to those who had the specific professional skills still required. The optimistic view of a decade earlier foreseeing *Canberra*'s role in Australia's coming fifty years of development, both internally and in terms of growing Pacific trade, was fading. The reality of her situation was that she was quickly becoming a liability whose only salvation lay in the possibilities of a then unstable and uncertain full-time cruise market.

In January 1973 *Canberra* was sent to New York, then seen as the hub of American cruise ship activity. There she would join Holland America's *Rotterdam* and *Statendam*, and the former *Hanseatic* (originally Zim's *Shalom*), then recently purchased by Home Lines and renamed *Doric*. All had been recently displaced from the line services they were built for. Also running weekly cruises out of the Big Apple alongside these was the Home Lines flagship *Oceanic*, an intended liner which had gone directly into cruise service upon her completion in 1965. *Canberra* found herself in strange company, far removed as she was from the Mediterranean, Australian and Pacific routes she and her crew were accustomed to. Perhaps strangest of all was that, in the absence of any P&O representation in New York, her cruises were being marketed through Cunard's facilities there.

While the Americans had been fascinated by *Canberra*'s futuristic outer appearance and impressed with the crisply modern decor of her lounges and bars a decade earlier, many were not prepared to book her great number of tourist class cabins lacking private toilet facilities. Quite simply, Holland America and Home Lines offered a higher standard of accommodation in this regard. Both Lines were already familiar with the American cruise market and knew what their passengers expected. *Canberra* was a newcomer with a surprisingly big cultural difference rooted in P&O's services half a world away.

Len Stuckey, who started as an assistant purser with Orient Line in 1949 and later moved to the sales and marketing side of P&O, felt that 'it was

*The Panama Canal's locomotive 'mules' stand by to take
Canberra in charge early in her career.*

very difficult to get Americans to understand
P&O'. While New Yorkers had been in love with
the old Cunard *Queens*, they and their compatri-
ots expected cruise ships of the 1970s to be of
the more modern and up-market image which
newer ships like *Sea Venture* and *Island Venture*
(later to become P&O's *Pacific Princess* and *Island
Princess*) then portrayed. They wanted the more
highly organised activities, smorgasbord dining
and the airline-style glamour of Scandinavian
cabin stewardesses.

After running a few lightly-patronised cruises,
*Canberra* was laid up off the South Carolina coast

for three weeks in the hope that bookings would
improve. When she did resume service in the
spring, her trading results were mediocre, despite
the casino which had been set up aboard and the
complete amalgamation of her first and tourist
class facilities. Her Caribbean itineraries were sold
at rock-bottom prices to cover costs in the hopes
of promoting the ship.

On 1 June 1973 came the announcement that
everyone had been fearing most; *Canberra* would
be permanently withdrawn from service in the
September of that year. Some were even afraid
that P&O might eventually get out of the passenger business altogether. The ship was proving to
be unsuitable for the type of operation P&O was
then aspiring to build up in the American market.
Early trading results from their first purpose-built

cruise ship *Spirit of London* which had gone into service on the United States West Coast that January were already encouraging, while *Canberra* was expected to show a £500,000 loss.

*Oriana* would become the flagship, with *Canberra*'s place in effect being taken by *Orsova*, a ship of already advancing age, some seven years older than *Canberra*. This was a solution which, in a purely business context, seemed to look right. *Orsova* was, after all, a smaller ship whose fewer berths would be easier to keep filled, and her slightly shallower draught gave her the flexibility to dock alongside at the many ports where *Canberra* either had to use tenders to get her passengers ashore or where she was denied access altogether on account of her deep draught. However, there were a number of other important factors which people who had shipping in their blood were able to visualise beyond the vicissitudes of business strategy. To many experienced P&O people, both at sea and ashore, *Canberra*'s disposal did not appear to add up at all.

Despite her deeper draught, they firmly believed that *Canberra* offered far greater potential as a cruise ship in the long run. *Orsova* was still an old-style Orient ship with vast amounts of cargo space which would at some time or another have to be converted into accommodation, as had been done at considerable expense in *Andes* as far back as 1959. *Canberra* had no such redundant spaces below decks, and already offered a wide range of cabin accommodation complemented by extensive public and recreational facilities which were more modern and of a generally far higher standard. Those who knew both ships also realised that *Canberra* was remarkably solid and well built, giving her the chance of a longer service life than *Orsova*'s altogether lighter construction might sustain.

At the corporate level, P&O had been re-organised and restructured on the basis of recom-mendations made by the management consul-tancy firm of McKinsey. In the shipping side of things, P&O's individual companies such as British India and New Zealand Shipping were division-alised. Passenger shipping, by then almost exclu-sively cruising, was organised into European, American and Australian sectors. The American entity was soon to acquire Stanley McDonald's Princess Cruises in mid-1974, retaining the name.

Clearly, *Canberra* was not the right ship for the American division, where many of the Caribbean ports could not accommodate her draught. She had grounded a number of times during the sum-mer of 1973. Likewise, she was no longer suited for the Australian market, where the emphasis for cruising was more on the South Pacific islands and Indonesia rather than her original Pacific-rim routes. However, Europe was different, with many continental, Mediterranean and Scandinavian ports able to accommodate her draught.

The executive board's position on *Canberra* had been handed down to the cruise divisions as a fait accompli. With this already announced to the world press, it would be extremely difficult at that stage to have the decision reversed without the board losing face. The European cruise sector's director, Peter Wise, set about with his staff to convince the executive board that the decision should nonetheless be overturned. Acting on what Wise calls his 'hunch factor', or that gut feeling which people have about things being right, a solid business case was presented for *Canberra*'s future in the British market. The executive body acquiesced, explaining to the press that they had since identified a growing demand for cruising in home waters for which *Canberra* would be better suited than *Orsova*.

While *Canberra* was winning her reprieve at P&O's new head office building in Leadenhall Street, the ship undertook one of the more unusual

*Waiting for the eclipse off the coast of Africa.*

and successful cruises of her career. Called the Voyage Into Darkness, this was an expedition to view one of the longest solar eclipses of modern times at its centre off the coast of West Africa on 30 June 1973. Among the special guest lecturers aboard for the 22 June - 8 July voyage were American astronauts Scott Carpenter and Neil Armstrong and the noted science fiction writer Isaac Asimov.

*Canberra*'s vast expanses of wide open deck were ideal for viewing the 5min 44sec total eclipse of the sun. Sun Deck became known as Tripod National Forest due to the huge assortment of scientific, optical and photographic equipment set up for viewing and recording the event. *Canberra*'s engines and much of her auxiliary machinery were stopped to keep her as still and as steady as possible while 2,600 guests, passengers and crew witnessed the cosmic spectacle.

*Canberra*'s passenger list for that voyage was as impressive as her roster of lecturers and other special guests. These included eclipse specialist Karl Ziegler, Nobel Prize-winning author Harriet Stratemeyer Adams and popular English author Nancy Drew.

There were hundreds of other scientists, teachers, artists, and other philosophers and creators from around the world. In fact, there was so much brain-power aboard, that when *Canberra* was called upon to rescue and treat a 63-year-old crewman with heart trouble from a nearby cargo ship, some of her passengers were able to help out. They managed to improvise a defibrillator using parts from a television camera, tripods, a calculator readout, a borrowed oscilloscope and various other items which on that cruise just happened to be on hand.

After completing her New York season, *Canberra* was converted for full-time cruising as a one, or 'open', class ship to take *Orsova*'s place for the 1974 British cruising season. Amalgamating the two classes was in itself simple enough since, like *Oriana*, *Canberra* was divided with first class in her forward half and tourist astern. Doors merely had to be opened amidships and deck barriers taken down. It was as easy as connecting the first and second class coaches of a train.

Some duplication of functions had to be dealt with. The first class children's room on Games

Deck became a card room, while the writing room off the William Fawcett Room was turned into a gift shop, leaving the Meridian Lounge annexe to fill its original function for all aboard. The Pop Inn, which had lost much of its following since families stopped migrating to Australia by sea, was made into the photographers' gallery. Changes to the cabin accommodation, including a permanent switch of the 140 convertible emigrant/cruise cabins to their two-berth mode with private toilets, reduced the ship's passenger capacity to a more manageable 1,737.

Perhaps most important, twelve of *Canberra*'s lifeboats were replaced with covered tenders to be used for ferrying passengers back and forth in those ports where she would have to lie at anchor. Boats 16 and 17 were replaced with portable landing stages which could be lowered as tender berths using the aft gangway hatches on D deck. While tendering is never ideal, these arrangements would at least make it as convenient and comfortable as possible for *Canberra*'s passengers.

The question about the conversion and its amalgamation of first and tourist class spaces which would only be answered by service experience

was, in Jim Davis's words, 'would it blend?' There was real concern that all passengers might converge on the Meridian Lounge, Bonito Club and Crow's Nest forward, leaving the former tourist class preserves lightly patronised. As it turned out, John Wright's original idea of designing rooms with different characters with which passengers identify themselves still worked, and even extended to Sir Hugh's first class rooms. As *Canberra* gained her reputation as a favoured British cruise ship through the remainder of the 1970s and on into the 1980s, her passengers developed a remarkable sense of place among her interiors. The Meridian Lounge remained a preserve of the more sedate crowd who listened to classical music, while families gravitated more towards daytime activities of the William Fawcett and Island Room. The Alice Springs, all by itself aft on B deck, remained a preferred spot for

*The Stadium Theatre Company prepare for the evening performance while the auditorium is empty.*

bathers and the Cricketers, as ever, remained *Canberra*'s pub and favourite 'watering hole'.

A professional cruise department, with a director, entertainment staff, port lecturers and a shore-excursion office, was set up. To the traditional liner-era diet of deck games, tournaments and competitions of one sort or another, horse racing and Bingo were added as well as professional evening entertainment and a variety of other activities. Variety and music-hall style shows were staged in the Stadium Theatre, while courses in such things as painting, crafts, and flower arranging were added to daytime programmes. Sequence dancing gained popularity, for participants and spectators alike. The port and general-interest lecture programmes were expanded, while *Canberra* continued to offer recently released films in her outstanding cinema.

These programmes were not merely a copy of

*A*n *art class in the Island Room before the room is transformed for tea time and the evening's dancing.*

Princess Cruises's offerings, but rather tailored specifically to the tastes of British passengers. The English-style bank holiday music hall programme was preferred over the Las Vegas-type revues offered by the Love Boats, and British clientele preferred to spend more time dancing and fewer hours gambling. The design of *Canberra* herself, with her magnificent all-the-way-round-the-ship promenade, shaded decks and wide open spaces topsides, always served the need of Britons who preferred to spend far more time outdoors on deck than their American counterparts.

*Canberra* managed to prosper at a time when a great many other liners converted to cruise ships eventually failed. She achieved the same sort of affinity and loyalty among her passengers as had her earlier fleetmates, *Chusan* and *Arcadia*, and the competition's *Andes* and *Caronia*. Her first year of Southampton-based cruising had coincided with the world oil crisis, which was the final blow that put many older ships out of business. Ultimately, *Canberra* was to also largely fill the void left in the British market by *Reina Del Mar*, the last of her old competitors. Popular as they were in their own right, none of these ships could compete with

*Dancing in the Peacock Lounge during the
late hours of the evening.*

*Canberra*'s scale, range of cabin accommodation
and diversity of modern facilities.

A P&O information release, entitled 'Your
Cruising Questions Answered', was issued to
answer prospective passengers' most likely queries
in the early cruising days of both *Canberra* and
*Oriana*. It advised that passengers could choose
between cruises offering either a greater number of
port calls or more days at sea, depending on their
preferences for touring or enjoying onboard life. It
suggested that *Oriana* and *Canberra* offered the
best opportunities for enjoying shipboard life, typically making as few as four or five port calls during
a fortnight's cruise. Also one's cruise could be
enjoyed at one's own pace, either as a quiet and

relaxing experience with a good book on deck and the smell of the sea air, or, as the copy put it, '..all the fun of the fair..', with planned activities and entertainments from early morning to late at night.

It clearly addressed the question of those looking for romance and companionship at sea, pointing out the tendency of people to be less inhibited on cruises that they might be at home on shore. Deck games and other activities were suggested as being a good way for passengers to get to know

*Ships have always been great places for meeting people, making new friends and finding romance, as discovered by William Whitelock Lloyd in 1890.*

one another. It was also pointed out that groups of friends who would tend to do things together on a cruise were often formed on the basis of their being seated at the same tables in the dining rooms. So far as romance was concerned, the release diplomatically went on to suggest that many passengers tended to fare well in making friends with their own, and the opposite, sex.

As far as getting to and from one's cruise was concerned, the release suggested that some passengers might prefer fly-cruise arrangements. They could fly from Heathrow or Gatwick to meet with their ship already in the tropics and avoid the Bay of Biscay crossing, which can be rough at any time of the year. However, if a passenger wished to have the full experience of

'(A) peculiar, though quite unintentional, way of striking up an acquaintance...'

'(Making) friends in the orthodox fashion...'

*C*anberra, *a vision of romance amongst the sailing boats and rising hills of Acapulco Harbour.*

sailing from a British port, it was pointed out that the crowded airports and long flights could be avoided in favour of being able to take the far larger quantities of baggage that the ship would allow over the airlines' restrictions. In those days 'boat trains' were still run from London's Waterloo station directly to *Canberra*'s berth in Southampton on sailing days.

As *Canberra* began to develop a following of repeat passengers, it was decided that these people should be given some sort of recognition through membership to a company-sponsored club. The idea had been tried successfully during the early 1970s in P&O's American cruise division before it became Princess Cruises. The club name changed from Captain's Circle to Cruisemasters, before the old P&O acronym POSH, which once supposedly designated Red Sea cabin preferences for Port Out Starboard Home, was eventually adopted. Len Stuckey inaugurated the British POSH Club aboard *Canberra* in November 1977, while the ship was steaming between Madeira and the west coast of Africa, signing up its first twenty-five members. The club has since grown to 22,000 members, including a Mr and Mrs Evans who have made all of *Canberra*'s world cruises in the comfort of one of her deluxe suites.

During those formative years of her exclusively cruising career, *Canberra* returned once more to New York, where she participated in one of the Liner events which the Port of New York organised in those years. On September 14 1978, she rendezvoused with *QE2* for a spectacular fly-over by Concorde. Since the Cunard flagship had been delayed by bad weather on the North Atlantic, the two liners met further out at sea than was intended, and it was possible for the supersonic jet to fly quite low between them, much to the delight of all aboard both ships.

*Canberra* made the headlines again in her 1979 season, when two fifteen year old schoolboys stowed away for an illicit Mediterranean holiday. They cleverly evaded detection for twelve days, managing even to go ashore in a number of ports without being in possession of travel documents or ship's boarding passes. Their fun was curtailed only when their parents reported them missing and the police asked for a search to be made of the ship.

Births are comparatively rare aboard cruise ships. However, during a Mediterranean cruise in the summer of 1981, a lady was diagnosed by *Canberra*'s doctor as being acutely pregnant. In the August, aboard *Canberra*, she gave birth to a son, Andrew Terry, who was given the middle name Biscay in commemoration of his place of birth. The family has since returned to *Canberra* for a cruise each year, with the hospital staff and crew taking a special delight in seeing Andrew grow from year to year, as, in a manner of speaking, an adopted son of the ship.

*Canberra* had begun to settle into the delightfully quiet sort of routine which *Oriana* had enjoyed ever since her maiden voyage and which shipowners dream about. But that was only to last eight years before her next adventure.

*Framed by palm trees,* Canberra *shines brightly in the tropical sunlight.*

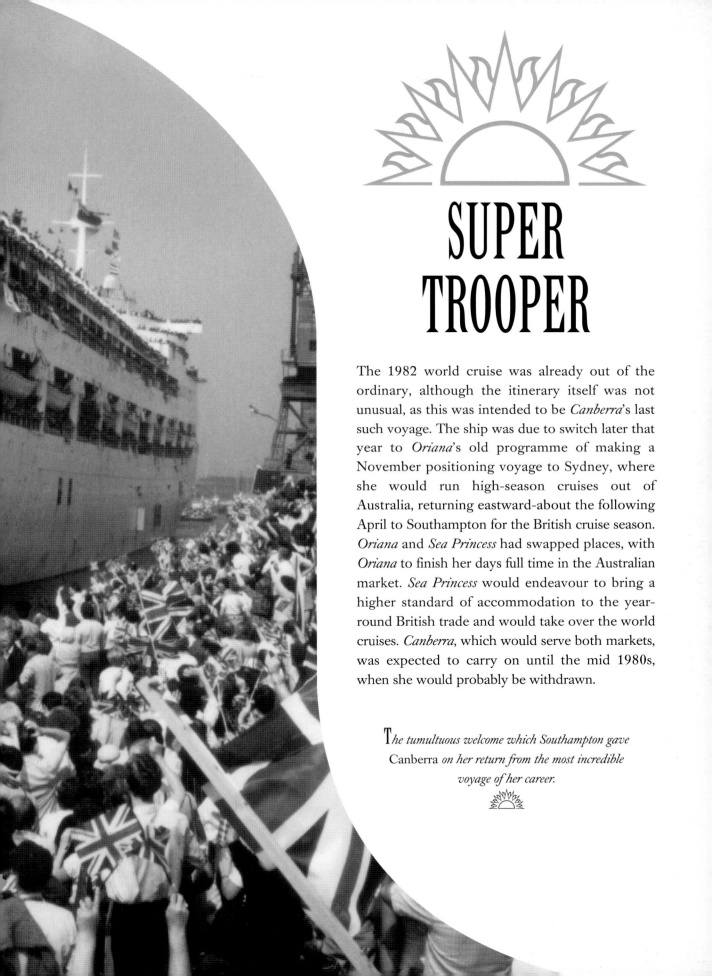

# SUPER TROOPER

The 1982 world cruise was already out of the ordinary, although the itinerary itself was not unusual, as this was intended to be *Canberra*'s last such voyage. The ship was due to switch later that year to *Oriana*'s old programme of making a November positioning voyage to Sydney, where she would run high-season cruises out of Australia, returning eastward-about the following April to Southampton for the British cruise season. *Oriana* and *Sea Princess* had swapped places, with *Oriana* to finish her days full time in the Australian market. *Sea Princess* would endeavour to bring a higher standard of accommodation to the year-round British trade and would take over the world cruises. *Canberra*, which would serve both markets, was expected to carry on until the mid 1980s, when she would probably be withdrawn.

*The tumultuous welcome which Southampton gave* Canberra *on her return from the most incredible voyage of her career.*

A *prelude to things which would unexpectedly follow as* Canberra *makes a rendezvous with* HMAS Canberra *on 28 January 1982.*

While all of this was fairly common knowledge throughout P&O and among their passengers, there were other events of world order whose implications were yet to be widely realised. While at sea ships have a remarkable ability to distance themselves from current affairs. To *Canberra*'s world cruise passengers, the little facsimile newspaper produced on board and the BBC World Service broadcasts which could be heard over cabin loudspeakers could just as well have been reporting events from some other planet for all their relevance to life aboard.

As *Canberra* sailed from Southampton on 6 January, the world as whole, let alone her passengers and crew, had scarcely noticed some minor rumblings of political disquiet coming from Argentina. The closest *Canberra* came to South America was to make her passage of the Panama Canal on 22 January. A few days later, as she steamed from Acapulco to San Francisco, there was an unusual event as the P&O ship met the Royal Australian Navy's brand new guided missile

frigate HMAS *Canberra*, then undergoing her sea trials and commissioning. The rendezvous had been arranged largely on the personal initiative of Mike Bradford, then *Canberra*'s relief captain, who was taking her as far as Sydney.

The two ships met in mid-afternoon on Thursday 28 January, as the Australian frigate joined the P&O flagship from ahead and took a position on her starboard side while Captain Bradford slowed his ship to 15 knots. HMAS *Canberra* closed in from 500 to only 100 yards, showing her impressive array of armament and radar antennae at very close range. A missile was run up into its launcher and one of the helicopters went aloft to shoot an 8mm film of the rendezvous. A heaving line was rigged between the two ships, for an exchange of letters and gifts to be made. The P&O liner sent a copy of the world cruise souvenir book, autographed by her senior officers and some P&O world cruise neck ties. The naval ship sent over a special bottle of Australian Chateau Tahbilk commissioning wine, and the

motion picture film shot from the helicopter. A letter was also sent to two delighted Australian entertainers, John and Alanah Cairney, who were working on *Canberra*'s world cruise.

At the beginning of the one-and-a-half hour rendezvous, Captain Bradford greeted the Australian ship with the words:

> To the Captain and ship's company HMAS *Canberra*, from the captain, ship's company and all passengers P&O SS *Canberra*.
>
> On this historic meeting of both *Canberras* may we wish you a long and successful commission. May the name of *Canberra* never be missed from the high seas and may the long connection between P&O and the Royal Australian Navy continue as those of our two great countries.

After the frigate had executed several manoeuvres around the P&O flagship Bradford thanked HMAS *Canberra*'s Commander B. Wilson:

> My thanks for your magnificent display and entertaining afternoon. To you all - Happy sailing, good hunting and a most enjoyable return to Australia. We look forward to our next meeting.

It was a historic meeting between a great passenger ship and a modern fighting ship. It had all been great fun, and probably nobody had the slightest hunch that within only a few months *Canberra* herself would be serving as a troop carrier and assault ship at war.

On 18 March, while *Canberra* was on her way from Colombo to the Seychelles, Argentine scrap metal dealers landed illegally on South Georgia, demolished an abandoned whaling station there and ran up an Argentine flag. By the time *Canberra*

was in the Mediterranean, Argentina had already invaded the Falkland Islands, and the United Nations Security Council had supported Britain's call for the immediate withdrawal of their forces.

While *Canberra*'s world cruise passengers were enjoying their last shore excursions in Naples, a hastily-called meeting had taken plce at the Admiralty in London to discuss the ship's range, speed, capacity and the possibilities of her being adapted for such things as helicopter support and refuelling at sea. P&O were told that, under the terms of an Order in Council to be signed by Her Majesty the Queen empowering the government to act in the crisis, *Canberra* was to be requisitioned to join a naval task force.

An advanced planning party boarded *Canberra* from a tug as she passed through the Straits of Gibraltar during the evening of Saturday 4 April, on her way home to Southampton. Among those who came aboard were Captain Bradford, who had been on shore leave since leaving the ship in Sydney and was called up in his capacity as a Royal Naval Reserve Officer. Their task was to plan the ship's preparations for military service in Southampton, arrange the removal of unrequired passenger and cruise materials and to allocate spaces for the various functions that would be needed by the task force. It was during those last three days of their cruise that *Canberra*'s passengers were brought back to the reality of world affairs.

As the passengers left the ship in Southampton on Wednesday 7 April, they were quickly followed by *Canberra*'s ten grand pianos, the one-armed bandits, much of her artwork and some furniture, including most of her deck chairs. Carpeting in the public rooms was covered with sheets of plywood to save it from the heavy wear and tear of combat boots. Later that same day, the Bonito Pool disappeared under prefabricated

*The assembly of the helidecks in preparation for national service with the Royal Navy.*

sections of a helicopter flight deck made by the nearby Vosper Thornycroft yard. Ceiling panels were stripped out of the Crow's Nest Bar, as the open observation deck above it was shored up to receive a second helipad. Another party of Vosper's men with cutting torches removed the railings and wind breaks alongside the midships flight deck. Below, the starboard-side baggage lift was secured at the Games Deck level so that its shaft could be used to take the oil pipes needed to refuel *Canberra* at sea. Boat 11 had to be taken out

*Still lying alongside Southampton's Berth 106, where she had disembarked her world cruise passengers,* Canberra *is hastily converted for service as a troopship.*

of its davits to make room for the RAS (Refuelling At Sea) gear.

Meanwhile vast quantities of stores went aboard until *Canberra* seemed as though she were straining at the seams. Containers were loaded on to the open spaces of Sun Deck aft, while ammunition was stowed in the wide covered areas aft on Games Deck, where the Lido Terraces have since been created. No-one could have imagined, when the ship was being planned, that such things as her spacious top decks and the practical feature of having a service lift directly accessible from the Promenade Deck would serve her in such good stead when she was used as a troop transport. It might also have seemed incredible that there would even be the need for trooping by sea in the day of the jumbo jet. However, the long sea distances and

*O*n *8 April, Her Majesty's troops start to embark; these are passengers who carry all their own baggage.*

*D*eparture at nightfall on Good Friday, 9 April, has the look of just another cruise until one notices that those lining the rails are uniformed military and naval personnel.*

lack of a suitable airport in the Falklands once again gave merchant shipping a vital strategic role in a time of crisis.

As *Canberra*'s conversion progressed at dockside, some 2,000 men of 40 Commando and 42 Commando Royal Marines and 3rd Battalion the Parachute Regiment were embarked. The ladies' hairdressing salon had become the Royal Navy ship's office and the William Fawcett shop was taken over as the Military Force commander's office. The Marines were given the photographer's shop as headquarters with '3 Para' nearby in the William Fawcett library. Use of the accommodation and public rooms was divided along the lines of the old class structure, with military officers and senior NCOs (non-commissioned officers) forward in what had been first class and other ranks aft in tourist. The Crow's Nest, with its ceiling tiles gone and having sprouted a grid of bare steel support columns for the flight deck above, became known as the Erection Bar. It was used as an officers' mess and was the venue for a number of band concerts.

Also embarking were a number of intrepid journalists who would keep Britain up to date with events in the Conflict both from *Canberra*, and later the Falklands.

A Thursday evening departure had to be postponed to the next day owing to late deliveries of some of the steel Vosper's needed for the forward flight deck. As darkness fell on Good Friday, 9 April, *Canberra* sailed for the South Atlantic, only three days after having landed her world cruise passengers. The forward flight deck had to be finished at sea by Vosper's workers who would travel with *Canberra* for part of the voyage. For some, such as Captain Bradford who had remained on board, there was the feeling that a political settlement would be attained before the ship reached Ascension Island. For others, like Peter Wise, who watched *Canberra* sail off into the darkness, there

was a feeling of foreboding, and the dread that some of those aboard might not return and that even *Canberra* could be lost.

*Canberra* was commanded by P&O's Captain Dennis Scott-Masson, with Captain Christopher Burne as the Naval Captain and Colonel Tom Seccombe as Military Force Commander. The ship continued to be run by her own crew, who had all volunteered to remain, albeit their numbers reduced to about half without the passenger services needed for cruising. One change made was that *Canberra*'s Indian and Pakistani crew were sent home, their places being taken by merchant marine volunteers. Only fifteen of the ship's company making the voyage were women, these mostly being in the purser's and medical departments.

*Canberra* was originally fitted out to serve both as a troopship and hospital ship, but much of the medical work was passed over to *Uganda* and other ships, as the dual role would not have accorded *Canberra* the full protection of a hospital ship under the Articles of War. Her facilities were only used to handle immediate casualties during the San Carlos landings and later to treat some of the Argentine prisoners of war during their repatriation voyage.

During the voyage south the embarked forces were kept busy in training exercises of one kind and another. Marines practised stripping-down and reassembling their automatic weapons until they could do it with their eyes closed. They had to learn the geography and topography of the Falklands and to be able to recognise landmarks and know their location ashore at any time without maps. Instruction was given in armed and unarmed combat tactics, communications, survival procedures and first aid. There were lectures and training videos to be taken in and committed to memory. There were drills on such things as helicopter assault training, vitally important in getting

*Captain Dennis Scott-Masson with his 'charge' before departure for the Falklands.*

combat forces ashore quickly and 'cross-decking' them to other ships as needed. No cruise staff could keep their charges as busy as those in charge on that voyage did. Ewen Southeby-Taylor, yachtsman, author and noted expert on the Falkland Islands was along as a 'port lecturer' of sorts, whose advice and counsel were to be of great value.

Physical training was of paramount importance, with the troops doing daily runs around the Promenade Deck in full kit and in step. These were quite memorable for the tremendous vibration they caused throughout the whole structure of *Canberra*, as the forces racked up a combined distance of 4,000 man-miles per day. It could be felt seven decks higher up on the bridge as well as below in the engine room. As *Canberra* passed through the tropical latitudes, troops were warned by the senior medical officer in a public address broadcast that it was a disciplinary offence to render themselves unfit for duty on account of sunburn - one of the most common shipboard medical problems suffered by regular cruise passengers.

On Saturday 17 April *Canberra* went alongside the Kissy Fuel Jetty at Freetown in Sierra Leone, where she bunkered and took on fresh water and additional stores. Among the items requested were fifty steam irons and ironing boards. 'Razor sharp' trouser creases and lots of 'spit and polish' were in order, as usual, for the forces on board. The engineers, who had to supply the hot water for showers and laundry and the electricity for ironing, noted that the commandos and paratroopers paid more attention to deportment than a normal shipload of cruise passengers normally would.

*The daily exercise route which shook the ship from top to bottom.*

Once the forward flight deck and an inclined stretcher trolley leading down to the Bonito Club hospital area had been finished the men from Vosper's left for home. From this point on, the P&O roll-on/roll-off ferry *Elk* would be *Canberra*'s faithful stores provider whilst she would refuel at sea from Royal Fleet Auxiliary tankers.

The commandos and paras lived in comparative luxury aboard *Canberra*. They occupied the regular passenger accommodation, which, apart from the removal of some occasional furniture, was not adapted like passenger ships during the Second World War for the much higher numbers of troops carried aboard. There was ample deck space and two swimming pools were still available for what little free time their training schedule still allowed them. Catering continued to reflect *Canberra*'s normal cruise standards, at least for the officers and senior NCOs. Other ranks 'messing' in the Atlantic Restaurant made do with self-service and had to take care of their own cabins.

When it was thought that perhaps food supplies were going down a little too fast, forces were restricted to a choice of fish or the main course instead of being offered both. While this was in effect for the two main dining rooms, it turned out that somehow the order had not reached the crew mess, where the two were still being offered. Nonetheless, everyone was happy and morale was high aboard *Canberra*, which among her Embarked Military Force soon earned the nickname 'Super Trooper', in addition to her more widely-known popular moniker 'The Great White Whale'.

One of the most difficult and, as it turned out,

time-consuming exercises was that of darkening the ship at night. While 'blacking out' the decks and public rooms was simple enough, it was the cabins which presented the greatest difficulties. Half-an-hour after sunset the order 'darken ship' would be broadcast. Watchers would then hang over the bridge wings looking along *Canberra*'s

*Sunbathing en-masse armed forces style on the spacious top decks designed for passenger enjoyment; note the stores containers to left and right.*

sides for the glow of cabin lights. Even those from inner court cabins were spotted and had to be darkened. The 'darken ship' duty officers of the three units on board would inevitably be called to the bridge during dinner. The ship's broadcast system would then be kept busy: 'The occupants of cabins C49, C52, D238... return there now and darken them.' Sometimes it took as long as three hours. It was not until *Canberra* had almost reached the Total Exclusion Zone around the Falklands that 'darken ship' could be completed quickly.

*Stimulus for the mind during the outward voyage; an informal game of chess among comrades in their cabin.*

*An official photograph aboard* Canberra *of military, naval, and P&O personnel.*

After leaving the Ascension Islands, where she had spent seventeen days preparing for action, *Canberra* went on to an active war basis. Among other things, this brought the civilian P&O crew under the Naval Discipline Act. Its rather severe measures and draconian punishments never had to be enforced against *Canberra*'s crew, who continued to be guided by a sense of duty and their own merchant service's normal peacetime code of conduct. By this stage *Canberra* was operating with all of her watertight doors closed, as she had become a front-line assault ship.

Just prior to the San Carlos landings, Military Force Commander Colonel Tom Seccombe broadcast an address to all aboard *Canberra*. He finished by saying:

> I would like to congratulate all of the members of the Embarked Military Force for the exemplary way in which they have behaved over the last six weeks. A great many people who are not connected with either the ship or the Military Force were quite needlessly apprehensive about a situation which placed 2,500 Marines and Paratroopers in a comparatively confined space for an extended period of time. Those fears, as most of us supposed they would, have proven quite groundless, due in no small part to the way in which the ship's company of the *Canberra* have looked after us. In return we will do all we can to look after them.

Two days before *Canberra* went into San Carlos two units, 40 Commando and '3 Para',

*After a longer stretch at sea than passengers would normally experience, troops go ashore at Ascension island for training exercises.*

were 'cross-decked' to other ships using military landing craft, leaving only 42 Commando to make their landing from *Canberra*.

Thursday 20 May was D-Day in the Falklands, as *Canberra* made her way into Falkland Sound, between the islands of East and West Falkland, and then into San Carlos Water early in the morning of Friday 21 May. It was here that her company first heard gunfire in anger as HMS *Intrepid* bombarded suspected Argentine positions on nearby Fanning Head. *Canberra* was afforded some protection against attack by the surrounding terrain, but she too fired in anger, launching her Army 'Blowpipe' missiles at a number of aircraft which came in too close, and landing 42 Commando, the reserve unit, in the middle of the morning.

Later in the day, after HMS *Ardent* was hit, *Canberra* embarked her survivors, who were taken to the Meridian Lounge where they were each given a large tot of rum and a can of beer, while their names were taken for the survivors' signal. Throughout the day *Canberra*'s crew were frequently warned to take cover as enemy aircraft continued to attack the naval ships. On one such call, while the commandos were disembarking, two dining-room waiters took cover under a table, not realising that there was a box of fused grenades on top of it. Despite these frequent interruptions the crew managed to de-store as much as possible from *Canberra* for the forces' use ashore and to start making the cabins ready for their next occupants.

Fright was a factor for everyone that day, notably no doubt for the many merchant crew serving in *Canberra*. Captain Bradford recalled that things were not as bad for those on the bridge, where he was, since at least they could see what was going on around them. For those inside the cabins, the galley and other working areas and the engine room, there was the sense of not being able to do anything, with only the sounds from overhead and the occasional shudder whenever there was a hit close by. Captain Burne made numerous broadcasts to keep everyone as well informed as possible but as Captain Bradford himself said, 'At least on the bridge if you saw one coming your way you could duck at the right time.' It was the lack of a sense of presence in the face of the situation that was probably most discomforting for those below.

*Canberra* left San Carlos, again blacked out, under the cover of darkness. She undertook two more missions in the Falklands. These included the transferring of the 5th Infantry Brigade units from *Queen Elizabeth 2* and, finally, a voyage to the Argentine mainland to repatriate prisoners of war.

*In this painting by Ronald Dean,* Canberra *holds her own in San Carlos Water, landing 42 Commando, embarking survivors of HMS* Ardent *and firing on approaching enemy aircraft.*

On 28 May the forces brought down to South Georgia on the Cunard ship were cross-decked to *Canberra* and brought to San Carlos on 2 June. By the end of the following day, after all forces were landed, *Canberra* was left with only 620 people aboard and very limited stores.

After the Argentine surrender, *Canberra* returned to San Carlos and then went on to Port Stanley, where she embarked an entirely new type of passenger - 4,167 prisoners who had to be carried under guard. More than double the ship's normal passenger capacity, these men had to be accommodated as well as possible in all available cabins below A Deck, which was reserved for the remaining British naval and armed forces personnel on board. Many of the prisoners were bedded down in the public rooms and even in some of the protected deck areas. These also included some wounded, who were taken care of in the hospital units in the Stadium and Bonito Club areas above on Games Deck.

The two greatest logistical problems were

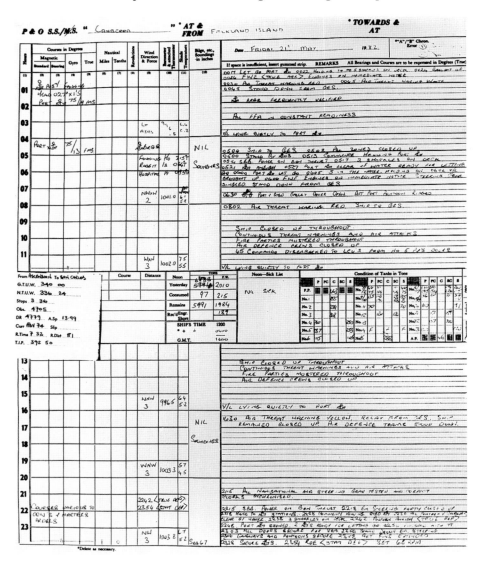

*Canberra's log from San Carlos Water on Friday May 21 1982.*

ack in San Carlos Water on 2 June, Canberra lands 5th Infantry Brigade which was transferred from QE2 at Grytvitken, South Georgia.

providing enough guards and feeding such a large number of people. Guards were needed at the end of each passageway and in all of the stairways, as well as in the public rooms and on the decks, requiring a force of 220 men. Only half that number could be provided by the detachment of Welsh Guards aboard, with the remainder having to be made up from Royal Marine bandsmen and any-

one else who could be 'press-ganged' into service. With the galley working flat out, the prisoners could at best be fed only twice each day in marathons of five sittings each, running from 06:00 to 11:00hrs and again from 17:00 to 22:00hrs. To help the ship's crew and guards keep track of their new charges, each prisoner had to wear on his clothing a regular cruise baggage tag, with the deck letter already printed on it and his cabin number handwritten in black ink.

After having been 'dug in' in the mud of San Carlos and Port Stanley, the prisoners were in dire need of hot showers. Each was given a bar of soap and a towel. For those in cabins without baths or showers, and the rest who had been berthed in the public rooms, the wash parade went on around the clock. Those in the Meridian Lounge filed down to the communal showers and baths on C deck, while their shipmates in the William Fawcett Room, Peacock Room further aft and above in the Alice Springs were taken above to B deck. While the continuous requirement for hot water was a concern to Canberra's officers, the engineers simply coped with this demand as they had with every-thing else asked of them. Criticised as Canberra's sanitary arrangements have often been in relation to her cruising role, in this unusual instance her 'public baths' indeed served her well.

Canberra departed from Port Stanley early on Friday 18 June, arriving a little more than twenty-four hours later at Puerto Madryn in Argentina. She made this voyage under international law as a 'cartel ship', engaged in the exchange of prisoners and in the role of carrying official communications between the two sides. As such, she would be accorded protection, on the understanding that she carried only one signal gun and did not engage in any illegal activities. As Canberra steamed into Argentine territorial waters at 10:06hrs on Saturday 19 June, where only weeks earlier she

*P*risoners-of-war were embarked by way of the ship's own tenders at Port William on June 16.

would have been fired upon, she was escorted by the Argentine Navy's *Santissima Trinidad*. By 13:00hrs *Canberra* was alongside, for the first time since leaving Freetown in Sierra Leone, on her way south nearly two months earlier, and ready to discharge her prisoners.

Once again, *Canberra* had experienced a new type of passenger who might have been troublesome. Apart from a few instances of cabins being fouled, and some mild signs of hostility in the demeanour of a few prisoner NCOs, there were few incidents. Two prisoners showed up in the engineers' workshop on G Deck after accidentally finding their way via an auxiliary staircase at the aft starboard end of the Atlantic Restaurant, mistakenly thinking it would take them back to their cabins on F Deck. They were not the first to make that mistake, which over the years had brought the occasional passenger to the same place. During the night, those bedded down in the forward end of the Meridian Lounge had apparently squeezed one of their smaller men through the gap at the top of the Century Bar doors unobserved by the guards. Once inside he had passed bottles of champagne and liquor out to his comrades, who distributed the booty throughout the Meridian Lounge by rolling the bottles along the floor. Amazed that any adult could get through the space, the crew later asked bar steward Peter Steele, who was quite slim, to try the same trick. He was unable to squeeze through the gap, and it was thought that this could have been an inside job done by shoreside personnel in the Falklands while de-storing medical supplies also stored in the Century Bar.

*Canberra*'s crew treated her Argentine 'passengers' with much the same courtesy they were accustomed to showing her regular cruise clientele. One prisoner later told a reporter from the German language magazine *Stern* that he had been very touched at being addressed as 'Señor', and when the crew were cleaning the cabins, they found in many of them notes which simply said 'Thank you'.

Whilst *Canberra* was returning to Port Stanley to pick up a second contingent of prisoners, it was announced that she would reload the unused stores taken ashore in San Carlos, embark all the Royal Marines from 40, 42 and 45 Commandos, and head home to Southampton. At 17:22hrs on Friday 25 June, *Canberra* weighed anchor and sailed for home with 2,489 Marines on board. It was a happy and jubilant voyage, which for the embarked forces served as a well-deserved period of relaxation and rehabilitation. Once *Canberra* was away from danger, Captain Scott-Masson sent a telegram to Dame Pattie Menzies in

*Argentine prisoners bedded down for the night on the floor of the Meridian Lounge.*

Australia to say that 'her' ship was safe and sound as she had always maintained an interest in *Canberra* and had been concerned about the ship's Falklands venture.

On 30 June blackout precautions were dropped, and later, on 3 July, *Canberra* passed five nautical miles south-west of Ascension Island. *Elk* rendered her last good deed to 'Super Trooper' in the form of desperately-needed supplies of beer, enough for everyone to toast the birth of Prince William to the Prince and Princess of Wales. The next day *Canberra* 'crossed the line' and was in the northern hemisphere. Captain Bradford recalls that while he was on watch during the last night of the voyage he continually heard periodic splashes

around *Canberra* as all sorts of loot or booty which the troops realised they would not be allowed to bring ashore went unceremoniously over the side.

On the bright and sunny morning of Sunday 11 July, *Canberra* returned home to what was reportedly one of the most tumultuous welcomes ever given to any British ship. Hundreds of small private boats and chartered craft came out to greet the 'Great White Whale' as she made her way up the Solent into Southampton Docks. The smudged and rust-streaked condition of her hull told the tale of her heroic deeds and of the fact that she had been at sea for a record ninety-four days during which she had steamed 25,245 nautical miles to latitudes as far south of the equator as Southampton is north of it. *Canberra*, and all aboard her, indeed had much for which to thank the unsung heroes of her engineering department. Unseen as they were for so much of their time

A *triumphant return home on 11 July as* Canberra
*approaches Southampton docks amid an armada
of small craft.*

aboard, those who toiled below the waterline in the heat and noise of the machinery spaces had not so much as flinched in their dedication to keeping *Canberra* and all her on-board services going the whole time.

The Fleet Commodore in Chief, Admiral Sir John Fieldhouse, Commandant General of the Royal Marines, Sir Stuart Pringle and Prince Charles flew out to *Canberra* to welcome home the

*As the military forces once again line the rails their jubilation is expressed in the signs hung from the ship's sides.*

ship, her company and the forces on board. The VIPs took their leave early, so that the ship herself and those aboard could savour the glory of the homecoming on their own. As *Canberra* neared her home berth, thousands were on the quayside to welcome husbands, daddies, sweethearts and loved ones. Southampton police reckoned that altogether some 35,000 people had poured through the gates.

*Canberra*'s gangways were swung into position at 11:00hrs. By 14:00hrs everyone was ashore and the ship lay empty, ready for the most extensive refit of her twenty-one year life, which would prepare her for her next cruise passengers.

*H*RH *The Prince of Wales greets Captain Scott-Masson after piloting his own helicopter out to meet* Canberra.

*A*s *Prince Charles' helicopter leaves the deck of* Canberra, *her company and embarked forces savour their final hour of glory as the ship comes alongside Berth 106.*

# CRUISES

In the weeks which followed *Canberra*'s return home from what one P&O press release referred to, with typical British understatement, as 'her unscheduled voyage to the South Atlantic', she was given a new lease of life. Over the following sixty-three days she underwent one of the most thorough refits of her entire career. Altogether this involved some 3,000 tasks, ranging from major items such as removing the two helicopter decks and dismantling the RAS gear, a complete overhaul of the main machinery and replacement of countless auxiliary items, to a thorough reconditioning of all accommodation and passenger areas. The work was done by Vosper's in Southampton.

On 9 August *Canberra* went into the King George V graving dock, where she spent three weeks. There, the heavy structural work of removing the flight decks was carried out, her underwater hull surfaces were cleaned and she was given a new coat of anti-fouling paint. Her main machinery, which her engineers had kept running so reliably the whole time, was thoroughly

*A horse-drawn cart approaches* Canberra *at one of the many port calls on her long route.*

overhauled. She was then returned to her home berth where the remainder of the work was completed.

One of the passenger lifts, which twenty marines had overloaded and accidentally sent into near-freefall to the bottom of its shaft, had to be repaired. Two completely worn out dish-washers in the galley were replaced and all of the washing-machines and tumble-dryers in *Canberra*'s passenger launderettes also had to be replaced. Ladies travelling after the Falklands would be able to wash their 'dainties' in machines they could be absolutely sure had never been used by commandos and paratroopers to clean up and dry their rucksacks, duffle bags and combat boots. Lavatories had to be repaired and thousands of tap washers needed to be replaced in cabin washbasins.

One important job in restoring the passenger areas was the replacement of worn deck and floor coverings. This work was sub-contracted to Durastic, a firm specialising in marine deck coverings. They in turn approached the Harefield Rubber Company, which had made the ship's floor tiles in 1960, for direct replacements of the original colours and patterns which had long ago been discontinued. The company agreed to put these back into production on special order for *Canberra*. Samples were produced for approval in only a few days and, over the following weeks, more than 2,000 square metres of tiles were delivered to Southampton.

Great care was taken to restore *Canberra* to her former interior architectural beauty. With very few exceptions, apart from the changes in room allocations made for cruising in 1974, the enduring work of Sir Hugh Casson, John Wright and Barbara Oakley was restored to its original character. Only the Island Room, which was never one of *Canberra*'s more inspiring interiors, was changed with the addition of a quadrangular sit-up bar on

its starboard side, and the introduction of a floral decorative scheme throughout. Another change, although more of a technical nature, was the addition of air conditioning units in the Stadium Theatre. These would be needed for the months when the ship was cruising out of Sydney, in the tropical heat of the Australian summer. With her facilities thus restored and enhanced, she had never looked better throughout her twenty-one years of service.

Nonetheless, *Canberra*'s long-term prospects were still uncertain. The fact that she was consigned to seasonal cruising in Australia was seen by many as an ominous sign that her days might well be numbered. No P&O ship in modern times had been kept in service for more than twenty-five years. An order already placed in Finland for a 40,000-ton cruise ship of radically new design, albeit earmarked for Princess Cruises as *Royal Princess*, seemed to indicate that P&O might well be looking to new directions in cruising.

*Canberra* resumed her regular commercial service on Saturday 11 September, taking up the last three cruises which had been on her original 1982 British season schedule. Her evening sailing time was brought forward to 13:00hrs so that full television coverage of her departure could be given in daylight. She was given a gala send-off as thousands again turned out to see her. They lined the shores, and followed in small boats and excursion vessels, including the veteran paddle steamer *Waverly*, whose saloon deck was all but awash as the old paddle steamer heeled towards *Canberra*, whose own passengers were lining the rails. As *Canberra* drew away from her berth, she was again serenaded by the Royal Marines Commando Forces Band, this time playing two numbers which were composed in her honour by director of music Captain John Ware. One of these was a march entitled 'San Carlos', and the second, written at the

*The strains of music from the Royal Marines Commando Forces Band waft up to* Canberra*'s decks from a sea of streamers at sailing time.*

request of *Canberra*'s Captain Scott-Masson, was named 'Orbem Cingit', the ship's Latin motto, meaning 'she circles the world.'

The Army Air Corps honoured *Canberra* with a helicopter fly-past, while other ships in Southampton Docks, including *Sea Princess* and the tiny Port Stanley-registered Atlantic survey ship *John Biscoe*, dipped their flags and sounded their whistles in salute to the 'Great White Whale'. *Canberra* was again taking up, as Captain Scott-Masson once put it, 'delightfully dull' cruising, in what was to be a veritable renaissance of her

career. Mid-afternoon her engines were stopped just off the Nab Tower, while her magnetic compasses were re-calibrated, a necessary step whenever significant structural alterations have been made to a ship. With this, the last vestige of her valiant 'national service' passed quietly into history.

The three remaining Southampton-based cruises were completely sold out, and *Canberra* went on to enjoy a successful Australian season over Christmas and the early months of 1983. One of her first visitors in Sydney was Dame Pattie Menzies, who had lunch on board with Captain Scott-Masson. She was no doubt pleased at the fine condition to which 'her' ship had been restored. However, as is the custom while based in Sydney, four officers of the New South Wales police were carried on board just to be sure that

Canberra *seen against the futuristic flowing lines of the Sydney Opera House.*

the passengers kept *Canberra*, her crew and each other in good shape. Elements of the Australian sense of humour, which occasionally runs to such antics as throwing deckchairs overboard or, on one or two occasions, setting off fireworks in the public rooms, needed to be kept in check with a little encouragement from the long arm of the law. For infractions of this sort, which jeopardise the safety of others aboard and that of the ship herself, passengers could be locked up and put ashore at the next port and flown back to Sydney, without a refund and with no recourse of appeal against the jurisdiction of the captain.

The following two years were among *Canberra*'s most prosperous as she enjoyed an increase in bookings of as much as thirty per cent, keeping her almost fully booked. This was partly due to some 'catching up' on bookings which were cancelled because of the Falklands voyage and where passengers had opted to cruise later. There

was none the less a fairly strong 'Falklands factor', which made many people anxious to breathe the air of the famous 'Great White Whale'. A small display of Falklands memorabilia had been set up in the forward lobby on sun deck near the radio station. A huge enlargement of a photograph showing *Canberra*'s triumphant return to Southampton from the Falklands was hung in the aft stairway lobby on the same deck. The Battle honours badge was also added above the bridge windows. These were tactfully located where they would be easy enough to find for those interested, yet far enough out of the way for anyone who might rather not be reminded of the war.

While she could only expect to trade on her Falklands glory itself for a limited time, those years nonetheless helped *Canberra* ultimately to assert her position as the foremost cruise ship in the British home market. This was achieved by continuing to build on the overall formula which had been introduced in her 1974 Southampton-based season. Where *Canberra* differed from other cruise ships, particularly those based in Britain, was that she offered an unusually wide range of cabin grades and a diversity of public and recreational facilities second to none. She was able to provide something for everyone, and enough space for all to enjoy themselves at their own pace without getting in one another's way. These things were key to the ship's success, as she catered for a fairly large cross-section of British society as a whole.

*Canberra* continued to flourish as a uniquely British institution, escaping entirely the 'Americanisation' which has set the tone throughout most of the cruise industry, in much the same way as the Americans have set worldwide hotel standards and spread their fast-food chains around the globe. As Peter York pointed out in his 'non-establishment' *Sloane Rangers' Handbook*, *Canberra* offered passengers a British holiday resort atmosphere with which they felt completely at ease and at home.

The wide range of activities and amusements offered on *Canberra*'s cruises indulged the indigenous British passions for cricket, pantomime and music-hall shows. These have kept alive an ephemeral link with P&O's own rich background in the era of the Raj, and have sated the deep sense of tradition that Britons have always so revered. In other words, while, for instance, the delightful Golden Lion pub aboard *QE2* fulfils the American passenger's expectations of the traditional British public house, *Canberra*'s Cricketer's Tavern was always 'the real thing' for a largely British clientele.

After seasonally shuttling between the British and Australian markets until 1986, *Canberra* was once again reinstated as the world cruise ship. *Sea Princess* was transferred to Princess Cruises, who in the meantime had moved into the larger tonnage league with the commissioning of the new, Finnish-built *Royal Princess*. *Sea Princess* ran Alaska cruises for the North American high season, moving for the winter months to longer Pacific cruises, similar perhaps to those originally envisaged for *Canberra* and *Oriana*, touching on Sydney, but largely catering to American passengers. Sadly, in 1986, *Oriana* was retired and sold to Japanese interests for use at Beppu in a static role similar to that of *Queen Mary*. *Canberra* was to remain, beyond the lifespan of any modern P&O ship, as the line's sole survivor of its traditional routes to Australia and the Far East. She would also serve for a number of years as the only P&O ship cruising out of Southampton.

With a steadily increasing rate of repeat business, *Canberra* was beginning to establish for herself the sort of club-like atmosphere which had prevailed a generation earlier aboard *Caronia* and *Andes*. However, her greater size and wider diversity of accommodation and facilities kept her in a less

*The make-shift stalls underneath Alexandria's concrete pier appear in stark contrast to the white superliner towering above.*

elitist category, with a far more diverse basis of public appeal. *Canberra*'s cruise season would begin in early January with a westward-about world cruise, lasting until the beginning of April. Through the summer and early autumn she would sail out of Southampton on two or three cruises to the Mediterranean, the Atlantic islands, then north to Norway and the land of the midnight sun, or into the Baltic and the Scandinavian capitals of Copenhagen, Stockholm and Helsinki. Then there would be a cruise around Western Europe and a last visit to the Mediterranean before her annual

overhaul in November. After two weeks in dry dock, usually at Southampton, the year would generally finish with a Christmas and New Year cruise, before she would be ready to commence her world cruise once again.

It was a routine which *Canberra* was to follow from then onwards, as she steadily gained popularity and built up a repeat business of some sixty per cent. Peter Wise's hunch had proved him and his colleagues absolutely right, and had turned *Canberra*'s fate as a losing proposition into a sound commercial success.

Of all her voyages, *Canberra*'s world cruises were always among her most popular. While the more expensive suites and deluxe cabins would be among the first to sell, accommodation would also fill up quickly for those who wanted to escape

from the cold and wet British winters. Berths could still be booked in lower-cost shared cabins in the same way they had been in the days of P&O's liner services to Australia and the Pacific. The whole three-month cruise could be had in one of *Canberra*'s four-berth 'friendly fours' without private facilities for around £3,000. Thousands of ordinary Britons were thus able to enjoy the luxury of round-the-world cruises which they simply could not have afforded on other Lines, where accommodation could not be booked on a shared basis.

With *Canberra* once again committed to the year-round British market, she was given another extensive refit, this time in Germany at the Lloyd Werft yard at Bremerhaven, during the autumn of 1986. Whilst there she was in the company of *Queen Elizabeth 2*, which was undergoing a full

*At anchor,* Canberra *waits for her passengers to return from shore excursions and shopping in Gibraltar.*

conversion of her machinery from steam to diesel power. *Canberra*'s refit, although not nearly as extensive as that of the Cunard ship, went well beyond the usual upkeep and remedial work done during her annual overhauls.

No matter how popular a ship becomes, she must inevitably undergo some changes to keep her popularity and to stay up-to-date with changes in lifestyle and living standards. She cannot altogether escape the influence of newer cruise ships or of the latest trends in resort life and even home accommodation. The Peacock Room, which had suffered the loss of its distinctive canopy ceiling even before

*Canberra* went into service, also lost its peacock tail-motif drapery in the process of being redesigned as a dual-purpose daytime general day lounge and the nightclub Neptune's. The Atlantic Restaurant was extensively refitted to give its vast area a more intimate feel. A full-service deck buffet was installed in the port side of the Island Room, opposite the bar which had been added starboard side in the post Falklands refit a few years earlier. The two rather under-used stretches of covered deck aft of the Island Room, where ammunition was carried to the South Atlantic, were turned into attractive glass screened lido cafés. On Promenade Deck, the William Fawcett Room was completely refurbished and renamed the Ocean Room, which had originally been its intended name during *Canberra*'s early planning. The Stadium Theatre was fitted with terraced seating and improved production facilities, bringing it as close as possible to the theatre standards of other purpose-built cruise ships.

Soft furnishings and colour schemes were changed to reflect the same pastel California palette introduced in Princess Cruises' ships starting with *Royal Princess*, and later applied throughout their entire fleet. Fortunately, this was done without disturbing *Canberra*'s more outstanding architectural features such as the Pacific Restaurant's decor and lighting schemes, the rich woodwork and panelling of her Meridian Lounge, Century Bar and spiral staircase. However, the addition of valances and curtains at the entrance to the spiral stairway and the Century Bar area, compromised the original idea of the room's flowing lines and sense of infinite spaciousness without really adding anything worthwhile to the decorative scheme.

These changes, along with the installation of carpet for the first time throughout the cabin corridors and alleyways, served to give *Canberra* a greater sense of luxury in keeping with many of the more modern cruise ships by then in service. However, their effect was generally a 'blue rinse' to enhance the character of the gently-ageing ship rather than a 'face-lift' endeavouring radically to change its basic ambience.

By 1987 *Canberra* had herself achieved a twenty per cent share of the whole British cruise market, including air-sea packages, and forty-five per cent of all cruises directly starting and finishing in British ports. Alice Lovely, who had travelled from time to time aboard *Canberra* over the years, started to cruise fairly regularly, preferring the late-season sailings around September, when the Mediterranean ports were less crowded and cooler. She had tried several other well-known ships but in her opinion, none had the same 'family' feel of *Canberra*.

The people of Belfast have always retained a great affinity for Canberra as *their* ship. Whenever cruising aboard her, they would be quick to make it known where they were from. Many would tell of having worked for Harland & Wolff building her, or at least of friends, neighbours or perhaps fathers who were there. They have always been immensely proud of their association with the ship, even if this was a matter only of having lived, slept and worked near her birthplace. It is a source of sadness that *Canberra* has not returned to Belfast, particularly to say goodbye in her last year.

After being named as Commodore following the Falklands voyage, Mike Bradford returned to *Canberra* in the late 1980s as her master for a number of years before his retirement. Whilst master he arranged another naval rendezvous, this time meeting up with the new HMS *Ark Royal* off Lisbon. The two ships steamed alongside at close range for fifteen minutes, before the Royal Navy jumpjet carrier resumed her voyage to the Far East and *Canberra* continued her cruise.

*The new Lido Café, which emerged from the 1986 refit, enlivened the formerly under-used deck spaces where explosives had been stored during the Falklands voyage.*

Commodore Bradford and *Ark Royal*'s captain, Mike Harris, had last been at sea together in the Falklands when HMS *Cardiff*, under Captain Harris' command, had escorted *Canberra* into Port Stanley to embark the Argentine prisoners.

In August 1989 Commodore Bradford hailed another captain, this time 35,000 feet aloft. It was the occasion of the inaugural non-stop flight between London and Sydney, made by the new long-range Boeing 747 Series 400 airliner *City of Canberra*. On *Canberra*'s behalf he sent a message to the Qantas pilot, Captain David Massy-Greene:

> Congratulations on your epic non-stop flight from UK, an event which will be remembered as another milestone in aviation history and for which all in P&O '*Canberra*' salute you.

*Canberra* made one of several rescues at sea to her credit while on her 1987 world cruise. She pulled the Jones family from the sea after their yacht had capsized and sunk on their

*Another Royal Navy rendezvous, arranged by Commodore Bradford, with* Ark Royal *off the coast of Spain in June 1988.*

round-the-world voyage in the opposite direction. Their 35ft ketch had been inundated by a heavy swell, forcing them to take to their self-inflating canister liferaft. As the great white hull appeared on the horizon, the family at first thought she was the Princess Cruises' ship which they had visited a few days earlier in Acapulco. They were brought to safety in one of *Canberra*'s lifeboats, and treated royally by crew and passengers alike. A portrait of the family and a fine photograph of their yacht were given to the ship as a memento of the great kindness that had been shown to them.

The world cruises continued to be extremely popular, and earned a steady following from those who wanted to spend the winter months going round the world each year. Because of the greater length of these voyages compared with other cruises, they were always reminiscent of *Canberra*'s early years when she was engaged in long line voyages to Australia and the Pacific. This gave passengers the time to build friendships among themselves and for them to get to know the ship and her crew as regular line passengers once did. Those who came aboard for segments of the world voyages were never quite on the same footing, being regarded more as passing guests might be in a private club. First-time world cruisers who showed promise of returning could find themselves being taken under the wings of the older hands as new members of *Canberra*'s unofficial world cruise club.

Eleanor Hibbert, a writer of historical novels published under several pen names, the best known of which were Victoria Holt and Jean Plaidy, was a regular world cruise passenger. She had first sailed with Orient Line aboard *Oronsay* during the 1950s, and seemed to have found that shipboard life inspired her. She always booked cabin C40, one of the large demi-suites amidships, which was specially fitted with a small wooden desk where she would work, using a portable manual typewriter. On one cruise she was disappointed to find that her little desk had been left ashore after a refit. It was eventually found, and sent on its way to *Canberra*'s next port call. Eleanor Hibbert eventually died at sea, during a cruise aboard *Sea Princess* in January 1993.

Audrey McGaw was a world cruise regular who refused to fly. She always boarded *Canberra* where she lived, in Tenerife, on the ship's last call there before the world voyage and remained aboard until the first call back there afterwards. Sometimes this kept her aboard *Canberra* for as long as six months. On several occasions she had to spend time at a hotel in England while the ship underwent her annual overhaul before the Christmas and New year cruise preceding the global circuit.

Long cruises and round-the-world voyages have always been a good way for people to get away from whatever may be troubling them ashore. On the 1992 world cruise *Canberra* welcomed one of her more flamboyant passengers, who boarded at Fort Lauderdale. Known to the British press and the police as Miss Whiplash, or Lindy St Clair, she was seeking to distance herself from a controversial sex scandal which had political implications. She showed up aboard the ship after her car had been found wrecked at the bottom of Beachy Head with an alleged suicide note in it.

The West Sussex police contacted Ian Gibb, then *Canberra*'s captain, and asked him to verify that the holder of a British passport with a specified number was aboard. Indeed she had boarded as Carla Davies, and was occupying one of the ship's top-grade suites, travelling with an entourage of two others whom she referred to as 'Auntie' and 'Brother'. When Captain Gibb told her that the police wanted to talk to her about the circumstances of her car being found, she told him, 'I've done nothing wrong – there are no yellow lines on Beachy Head'.

As it turned out, she had arrived at a time when *Canberra* was to spend several days alongside the pier undergoing repairs to a damaged propeller shaft bearing. Miss Davies' presence took some of the pressure off the ship, as the press became far more interested in catching up with her. Passengers who went ashore were offered large sums of money by reporters for their boarding passes but, alas to no avail. Miss Whiplash had been asked to remain on board while *Canberra* was at Fort Lauderdale which, under the circumstances, she was quite agreeable to.

She had asked at the Bureau if there was anywhere she could sunbathe topless on the ship's decks and was flatly told, 'No'. At Acapulco, she went ashore for the day, hired a small speedboat and water-skied topless past *Canberra*'s anchorage. Later on during the voyage, she and her entourage went down to the Pacific Restaurant in the small hours of the morning, where she seated herself at the captain's table. There she stripped to the waist, put an officer's hat on her head and had her photograph taken, verifying that she had indeed been topless at the Captain's table aboard *Canberra*. She auctioned off a kiss to Captain Gibb at the ship's White Elephant Sale, netting a substantial contribution to seamen's charities. Carla Davies never joined *Canberra*'s world cruise regulars, but unexpectedly did turn up on the new *Oriana*'s maiden voyage in 1995.

'I think Miss St Clair wants to play deck quoits with
you again, Desmond.'

'There was no need to dress for the captain's table, Miss Whiplash,
everything on the *Canberra* is terribly "enformale".'

*Miss Whiplash unwittingly brought* Canberra, *once again,
to the attention of Britain's cartoonists during
the 1992 world voyage.*

During the 1994 world cruise *Canberra* again
became a rescue ship, this time off the west coast of
India. After leaving Bombay she received a 'MAY-
DAY' call from the German tanker *Stocidi* asking for
medical help for survivors which she herself had
picked up from the lifeboats of another tanker that
had suffered a vapour flash explosion. The nine
men were very seriously burned, and two had
already died aboard *Stocidi*. Two more perished
during the transfer by tender to *Canberra* and a further two more died aboard *Canberra* despite the
medical staff's efforts to save their lives. The
remaining three men survived, later being helicopter 'med-evaced' from *Canberra* in the Gulf of
Aden by the French Foreign Legion at Djibouti.

Later that year *Canberra* made one of the
shorter, but more memorable, cruises of her
career. She was made available for charter to the
British Legion for the fiftieth anniversary D-Day
commemoration over the weekend of 4 and 5
June. Fully booked, with many veterans of the
Normandy landings and their families aboard,
she and *QE2* both participated in the Spithead
Naval Review. The two liners then followed the
Royal Yacht *Britannia* across the Channel to
Normandy. Divine Services were held aboard
*Canberra* taken by the only surviving chaplain
from the Normandy landing and Captain Gibb. A
Lancaster bomber flew over and released one
million poppies from her bomb bays onto
*Canberra*'s decks. Rory Smith, who was aboard as
deputy captain, recalled that it was a magnificent
hit, with most of the flowers landing on the decks
where they were eagerly picked up to be treasured
souvenirs of the memorable occasion.

This was the most emotional voyage of Ian
Gibb's life. The feelings no doubt of most aboard
were summed up in the words of Gilles Pioeteyry,
the French pilot who took *Canberra* into
Cherbourg, who wrote the following words in the
Captain's visitor's book: 'Very happy to be on such
a nice ship and to meet the very sympathetic
Captain's family.'

*Canberra*'s full complement of veterans and
guests went ashore early on Sunday to take up
their positions on the beaches of Normandy for
a full day's programme of events. The whole

*A special service of Remembrance is held on board to commemorate the 50th anniversary of the D-Day landings in Normandy.*

observance was an unqualified success, entirely without mishap, a remarkable feat in view of the advancing age of so many among those aboard. While the first San Carlos landing was regarded as *Canberra*'s 'finest hour' in the Falklands, for those recalling their landings of the Second World War, the D-Day anniversary must surely have been her most memorable hour.

In April 1995 *Canberra* was to meet the brand new *Oriana*, newly arrived from her German builders, Meyer Werft of Papenburg. *Canberra* was about to sail on one of her Mediterranean cruises, while the new ship prepared for her maiden voyage under the command of Ian Gibb, promoted to Commodore to mark the occasion, as *Canberra*'s first master, Geoffrey Wild, had been for her maiden voyage thirty-four years earlier. What was perhaps most remarkable about this meeting of the two ships was that one could clearly see in the new vessel that she carried the influence of *Canberra*.

A *million Flanders poppies are released with remarkable accuracy from the bomb bays of a vintage Lancaster bomber.*

A *memorable voyage for* Canberra *and the flotilla of vessels
that accompany her on the D-Day anniversary.*

# A SHIP IN HAND

By the mid 1980s *Canberra* could certainly be seen as having lived up to her claim of being 'the ship which shapes the future'. Of all the new ideas in passenger ship design which have come into being since the early days of her planning, it is *Canberra*'s unmistakable image which has been the most prevalent. Variations of her profile with funnels aft were soon to appear in examples such as the Italian-flag *Oceanic* and *Eugenio C*, which were completed during the first few years of her life. These ships also featured lower-than-usual lifeboat arrangements, while *Oceanic* was even fitted with the same type lateral-boom cargo transporters.

*Eugenio C*'s funnels were remarkably similar to *Canberra*'s twin stacks, and her public rooms featured a stunningly attractive open plan, with a vista along the centre of the ship clear from the funnel casing through to the panoramic windows in the forward wall of the superstructure. Her stairways, lifts and other 'core' services were divided to either

*A detailed study of* Canberra*'s superstructure reveals her timeless elegance and gentle streamlining although the style of the small cabin windows above the boats belies her advancing age.*

*Canberra's funnels, romantically silhouetted against the sky at dawn, still held the power to influence her successor more than three decades later.*

side of the ship rather than being lined up along the central axis. Somehow *Canberra's* designers missed out on the opportunity of doing something similar.

By virtue of her approach to providing outer cabins with windows for all passengers, the 1984-built *Royal Princess* also featured a lower lifeboat arrangement and promenade deck encircling the ship at the base of her superstructure. At about the time *Canberra* was undergoing her 1986 refit, early renderings of Sitmar's third-generation cruise ships showed a distinctively stylised adaptation of the P&O ship's overall arrangement with fully-nested lifeboats and a three-quarters aft funnel. Ironically, with the subsequent take over of Sitmar by P&O, this ship, and two slightly larger sister ships, were all to be delivered in the early 1990s for service in the Princess Cruises fleet, becoming *Star Princess*, *Crown Princess* and *Regal Princess*.

Although these ships did not feature *Canberra's* 'walk-around' promenade, they did offer her below-the-lifeboats main run of public rooms and informal recreation deck spaces, both indoors and out, atop their superstructures. While specifically designed for an American-style cruise lifestyle, their layouts were able to bring a good degree of *Canberra's* flexibility to Princess Cruises' operation.

At about the same time that these ships were originally being planned for Sitmar, P&O Cruises was also engaged in some planning of its own for its European division. A new ship was not necessarily foreseen as a replacement for *Canberra*, but anything new would have to offer some degree of fleet identity and operational compatibility with her. *Canberra's* advancing age also had to be taken into account against the reality that any new ship would, as a matter of course, be in service after her inevitable retirement sooner or later.

As explained by P&O Cruises' marketing director, David Dingle, a cruise line always needs to have new cruise ship ideas in hand. There are many factors which can influence the opportunities

to build, including international exchange rates, shipyard delivery times, the availability of special financial arrangements and government subsidies and, alas, the slim possibilities of having to replace a ship lost to the perils of fire, sinking or even terrorist attack.

It was against this type of background that P&O launched its Project Gemini in 1988. At its inception this loosely envisaged a cruise ship of around 50,000 tons and a passenger capacity of between *Canberra*'s figure of 1,737 and 2,000. The projected ship was also to retain *Canberra*'s most popular characteristics and offer a more up-to-date version of her broad range of accommodation grades. It would be a ship in hand which could be built whenever the right circumstances prevailed or an urgent need arose.

Already assured of the influence that *Canberra* had asserted in the design of other ships, including *Royal Princess* and the then unnamed Sitmar vessels, the Project Gemini design team took a close look at those aspects of *Canberra* which contributed most to her remarkable public appeal.

At first it seemed difficult to pin down the essence of *Canberra* in terms of tangible features of the ship herself, but what eventually emerged was that it was not only her great diversity of facilities which made her work so well, but the fact that they still imposed a vestigial remnant of her original two-class structure. Those who booked the more expensive cabins which were once the exclusive preserve of first class, still continued to gravitate towards the quieter and more sedate ambience of the Meridian Lounge, Century Bar and Bonito Club. The often younger people who occupied the less-costly rooms originally belonging to tourist class tended to favour the more animated lifestyles of the corresponding lounges and other public areas. The Gemini people struck again on John Wright's original ideas of everyone finding places

they could identify and feel comfortable with, and where they would be most likely to find like-minded shipmates. As there was no longer any barrier between classes, the British social structure was retained in *Canberra* in much the same way it worked ashore. Everyone was free to find their own level socially without necessarily being confined by their outlay for cabin accommodation. It was a fine point of unofficial shipboard protocol or etiquette which would not apply in, for instance, the American cruise market.

They also found out that any new P&O cruise ship built exclusively for the British market should also retain *Canberra*'s walk-around promenade and her two separate runs of public rooms. However, it was thought that the main suite of rooms should be extended up into the deck above, using the space between the lifeboats. This would make use of an area not ideally suited for cabins for those rooms where an outside view is not important. There would need to be an elegant room equivalent to the Meridian Lounge for classical music concerts or conversation. There would have also to be somewhere like the Bonito Club or Neptune's for night-club entertainment and dancing. The dance floor here would also need to have a definite and easily visible edge, which is very important for sequence dancing.

The Cricketer's Tavern, Century Bar and Crow's Nest would have to be brought forward in larger and perhaps more sophisticated renditions which would still retain their essential ambience from *Canberra*. Also there would have to be some sort of homage paid to the spiral staircase. The new ship would also have to show some elements of *Canberra*'s exterior styling. Twin funnels reflecting similar style and mass would be ideal, and the thoughtful feature of providing an outer promenade beyond the glass windscreens of the upper decks would be expected too.

Obviously there would not be the same long foredeck of *Canberra*'s profile, and the more stocky form of modern 'economy of scale' cruise ships would have to be accepted as a matter of course. The Gemini ship would have to offer many of the features passengers would expect of any new ship. There would certainly need to be an atrium and, of course, cabins with their own private verandas. Modern lifestyles would also demand elaborate health and beauty spas and fitness facilities.

One feature of *Canberra* which would not be repeated was her popular and distinctive court cabins. Their attractive plan was in reality an oddity of liner-era design and only made possible by the highly labour-intensive custom-building techniques of her time. Cruise ship design has since come to stress far larger modularised and prefabricated cabins laid out on a simple plan with direct entry from a single pair of full length fore and aft passages.

The first calls for building tenders went out towards the end of 1989. More development work was done, and it was two years before an order was finally placed in Germany with Meyer Werft of Papenburg. To be named *Oriana*, the new ship was to be of 67,000 tons, and would offer accommodation for 1,760 passengers, expandable to 1,975 with all upper Pullman berths used. Details of her design and building were released in a series of ten magazines published at regular intervals during her building, somewhat similar to the way *Canberra*'s building progress had been fed to the public in her day. Although a ship of distinctive design in her own right, the influence of *Canberra* was abundantly clear in many of *Oriana*'s features.

*The superliner's rounded stern, which, although beautiful, would not be used in the design for Project Gemini.*

Inside, she would have a cricket-theme pub, named Lord's Tavern and inspired by Lord's Cricket Ground in London. The Curzon Room would be Meridian's equivalent and Anderson's would provide a special club-like atmosphere on a larger scale than *Canberra*'s Century Bar. The new *Oriana* would have her own Crow's Nest high up at the front of the ship and in, addition to her Oasis health spa, would offer spacious deck areas with football, cricket and golf nets, along with two recessed swimming pools atop the superstructure and a third pool aft and lower down near the main public rooms.

The new *Oriana*'s well-articulated interior layout was planned to give the same flow of movement among the ship's public spaces, cabin areas and open deck areas. The diversity of accommodation and public facilities would suit various functions and tastes, endeavouring to retain the essence of what the author of *The Sloane Rangers' Handbook*, Peter York, once described as a 'disaggregation of space', which he attributes to being the secret of *Canberra*'s success.

The architects and designers who would work on *Oriana*'s interiors and external styling were given short familiarisation voyages during segments of *Canberra*'s regular cruises in the early 1990s. Among these were the noted Swedish ship designer Robert Tillberg, and London-based British architect John McNeece. Both were well-versed specialists of cruise ship design, with Tillberg's early experiences having included the interior design of Swedish American Line's *Kungsholm*, by now cruising as *Sea Princess* for P&O. John McNeece had been among the original group of young British architects selected by Lady Brocklebank to design interiors for Cunard's *Q4* liner back in the early 1960s before the design approach was changed and the ship completed as *QE2*. He has since gone on to design passenger

Elevated to the status of a
full-service lounge from its
original status as an
enclosed lookout, the Crow's
Nest would be expanded in
the new Oriana.

spaces for some of the world's best known cruise ships. The cruise industry has produced a number of such outstanding specialists in the field since the days when *Canberra*'s designers had to be selected on the basis of their land-based work and very limited ship design experiences.

Robert Tillberg was very interested in *Canberra* and her workings and appeared to take a personal liking to the ship. Ian Gibb recalled that Tillberg seemed to be remarkably comfortable with his work, and that he approached it with a great deal of sensitivity and attention to detail. He particularly admired *Canberra*'s wide promenade, indeed one of the most handsome decks of its kind on any ship, and her tall twin funnels. He tried to stress both features as closely as possible in the new ship, as far as the technical constraints of modern cruise shipping would allow. While approaching *Canberra* from a tender at Tenerife and seeing her broadside floating at anchor, he was also struck by the attractiveness of her gentle streamlining. He took very special note of this in the shaping of the lifeboat openings with their raked stanchions.

John McNeece also seemed quickly to pick up an affinity for *Canberra*, no doubt stemming from a fascination with shipbuilding he gained as a child, albeit on the Clyde rather than on Queen's Island. He was particularly intrigued with the Cricketer's Tavern, managing to convey its essence to the corresponding space he created aboard *Oriana*, bringing to bear his own personal love of the game. One of his specialities lies in planning the flow of activities in the spaces he designs. In reshaping the Cricketer's long railway-carriage-like plan into the greater rectangular area of Lord's, he managed to give the room greater flexibility and diversity of function.

The new ship emerged with the characteristically heavier profile of the modern-generation cruise ship. Of necessity her lines of form were stockier in concession to the vast volume of internal space needed for the economy-of-scale proportions of larger cabins, more public spaces and extended supporting services of one kind or another. *Oriana* emerged without some of *Canberra*'s fineness of line, having perhaps more the stance of a Bentley than a Ferrari.

The need for exhaust economisers and energy-reclaim facilities for economical running and for silencers and filters to satisfy stringent environmental protection measures, has made a thicker funnel

*Canberra's original deluxe accommodation maintained its lustre over the years with only nominal upgrading of soft furnishings and fittings.*

necessary. While cleverly contoured to look like twin stacks close-astride the centre line from each other, the two outer shells are in effect 'webbed' together across the centreline by a housing necessary to contain the extensive inner workings. It had been hoped that this connecting element could have been a lattice work of steel tubes, like the funnels on some of the latest Princess cruise ships. Another suggestion was that it might be painted black, 'dodging' its existence behind the illusion of a sort of *trompe l'oeil* shadow effect.

Yet in these lines of form and scale of proportion, elements of *Oriana* could immediately be seen as being descended from *Canberra*. The plated-in deck with regularly-sized windows above the lifeboat recess gave a similar balance of the hull and superstructure masses and the same visual separation of the lifeboats and the open decks above as contributed so successfully to the earlier ship's distinctive image. The gently swept-back form of the lifeboat openings themselves bore Robert Tillberg's impression of *Canberra*'s attractively subtle streamlining. The arrangement of the lido deck, with its glassed-in promenade encircling the health and beauty complex, reflects an up-to-date adaptation of *Canberra* top deck windscreening with its unique outer promenade area.

Although concealed at its forward end within the superstructure plating, the open Promenade Deck loop beneath the lifeboats was carried all the way around the ship, as in *Canberra*'s plan. Once again, the mass of the funnels was visually balanced against a deckhouse extension forward. Here, too, this is set back from the forward end of the superstructure proper, providing a spacious observation deck forwards. This was designed to house the forward-facing health spa, and at its higher level the Crow's Nest, with *Oriana*'s bridge being located below these lofty outlooks in the upper forward end of the superstructure proper.

Aboard *Oriana*, passengers would find a same-scale rendition of *Canberra*'s famed spiral staircase joining the two levels of her Selfridges shop, and that the Curzon Room offered a worthy equivalent to the Meridian Lounge's quietness and elegance. Despite the presence of such modern features as the inevitable atrium, the now *de rigueur* fitness spa and most welcome addition of a full-size theatre, *Oriana*'s designers had endeavoured to keep the general feeling of intimacy and human scale of

*Canberra*'s public spaces. This was given a high priority in maintaining the earlier liner's acquired club-like atmosphere on the new ship's larger scale. *Oriana*'s designers thus resisted any urge to glorify the expression of vastness in favour of expressing elegance and good taste.

The ability of *Canberra* to have such a strong influence over the building of a ship so far into the future was truly remarkable if not absolutely unique in the history of modern shipping. During the passage of three decades of her career, when even her own future was at times in jeopardy, she managed gracefully to make the transition from line service to full-time cruising. This was accomplished with remarkably little structural change and a seamless blending of her two passenger classes in a manner which, rather than creating discord, actually built on her diversity of character as a cruise ship. Although never intended to meet the superlative standards demanded on North

W*ith the funnels, gentle streamlining and other features of* Canberra *Robert Tillberg so admired, the new* Oriana *is seen as a worthy successor.*

Atlantic line services or in the mainstream American-based cruise market, she nonetheless succeeded not only in keeping but in setting the pace of developments in the British market.

*Oriana* is still a very new ship, but after two years of service seems to be off to a very good start. Thanks to *Canberra*'s outstanding design and long standing structural endurance she has been given a living legacy upon which to build her own following and successes. The great care that has gone into her unique design and solid construction have brought that already acquired margin of success fully up-to-date with current cruising and lifestyle trends and, above all, with the highest safety standards.

As a whole *Oriana* is, however, a ship of a more modern concept and must ultimately build up her own loyal following over the years, as has *Canberra*. No doubt in time she will achieve this, but for the first years, particularly after *Canberra* has gone, she will have to overcome the inevitable prejudices of those whose loyalties to the old ship will live on in their hearts. As *Oriana* inevitably builds a devoted following of her own, she will gradually in due course also win over those who grieve the parting of *Canberra*.

# AT HOME ABOARD CANBERRA

When Ian Gibb walked up the gangway to take his place as *Canberra*'s staff captain in 1977, he said he felt immediately at home. He had instantly discovered the same attraction that this ship had held for many of her passengers, officers and crew over the years. *Canberra* has always been uniquely British in that very special sense of good-humoured friendliness and the wholesome domesticity of everyday life in the United Kingdom. It is a sense of belonging to and feeling part of something very comfortable and enduring.

The mediums of film and television have on occasion brought *Canberra* into the lives and homes of many people on both sides of the world.

*At anchor, gangways and portable landing stages rigged,* Canberra *appears as thousands of passengers have seen her on their return from shore excursions.*

Cruise to the sun in P&O's Canberra
-the James Bond ship
as featured in 'Diamonds are Forever'

A *P&O advertisement following* Canberra's *appearance in the James Bond film* Diamonds are Forever.

Some scenes of the James Bond film *Diamonds are Forever*, were filmed aboard the ship early in her career. BBC television did a show with *The Two Ronnies* aboard the ship and, at the time of writing, an episode of *Melissa* is scheduled to be filmed on board. In the 1980s, Sir Jimmy Saville, who has been a regular passenger with P&O over the years, arranged for a young girl to experience life as a crew member aboard *Canberra* as part of his television show, *Jim'll Fix It*. In addition to these cameo appearances, *Canberra* was given extensive coverage on British television on her return home from the Falklands and on her D-Day anniversary cruise to Normandy in 1994.

*Canberra* earned the reputation of being a very friendly ship, where people knew their way around and were familiar with her crew, which was fairly stable with many people at all levels who had served long periods with the ship. The design of the ship herself helped, with its original warm colours and rich hues remaining largely intact. Even the layout helped, since *Canberra*'s way of doing things tended to bring people together and give them opportunities to meet and mix. Passengers would walk through many of the public rooms to get from one place or activity to another, affording them the opportunity to meet new friends and renew old acquaintances. Perhaps the cabaret artists were not so happy to have people passing through the rooms while they were rehearsing during the daytime but, as Rory Smith once pointed out, *Canberra* was never planned for them.

The cabin courts were remarkably popular and provided further opportunities for people to meet and socialise. They created a neighbourhood focus for people in the adjoining cabins to meet for pre-dinner drinks or informal parties. Unfortunately, the rationale of modern modularised accommodation arranged along featureless stretches of corridor does not support this sort of contact among adjacent cabin occupants. At the same time, many of *Canberra*'s original tourist cabins aft were small and only the more expensive rooms received television in 1987, encouraging passengers to spend more time on the decks and in the public rooms.

Over the thirty-five or so years of her life, *Canberra*, her captains and ship's companies have made many friends around the world. She has engaged people in all walks of life from all parts of the world, and has done so both in peace and war. Recalling some of the first class passengers on early line voyages, Captain Jock Lefevre said, 'There were those who travelled first class, and there are those who were first class'.

While being invited for drinks with Captain Lefevre during one voyage, Lord Kemsley noticed that the master was drinking Victoria Bitter, a beer which was not sold in *Canberra*'s bars. Captain Lefevre explained that it was his personal favourite, and that he always arranged to have it sent to the ship for his own use. Nonetheless, he offered it to his guest. As the two men became friends the special beer supply ran down much faster than it normally would have, and the captain fully expected to run out before the voyage's end. Later, while the ship was in Colombo, Captain Lefevre received a call from his steward, asking, 'where do you want 'em, sir?'. Without a word to the captain, Lord Kemsley had discreetly gone behind the scenes, found out what arrangements needed to be made, and had ordered enough of the favoured brew to see the two men through the rest of the voyage.

OVERLEAF

*A painting by Tim Thompson depicting* Canberra *as she accompanies the Royal Yacht* Britannia, *also being retired in 1997, to Normandy as part of the D-Day anniversary in 1994.*

*Always a popular ship with the Australians, Canberra has spent a number of seasons cruising out of Sydney, where she is seen here against the evening sky and the Harbour Bridge.*

On another voyage, in 1964, Sir Donald and Lady Bradman travelled aboard *Canberra* with their son John, who was then a teenager. The youngster wanted to arrange a small party for some of his shipboard friends while his parents were ashore for the evening in Colombo. Lady Bradman had asked Lefevre, who was then deputy captain, to keep an eye on the gathering, explaining that a record player had been borrowed from one of the ship's hostesses, and that the party had been allowed on the understanding that there was to be no alcohol and not too much noise. When Lefevre looked in on the gathering about mid-evening he shook his head disapprovingly at the smell of rum from the glasses of pop and motioned for the volume knob be turned down a notch or two. Nothing more was ever said, and the party eventually wound up without incident,

save perhaps an undisclosed adolescent hangover or two the next morning.

The many thousands of others who travelled to new lives on the other side of the world, in Australia and New Zealand, during those years had the times of their lives and developed their own special affinities for *Canberra*, though in most instances these were one-time passengers. The Mchugh family were perhaps typical, making the most of their voyage on *Canberra* as an interlude of joy and relaxation before setting about the hard work of setting up their new home. They took tours by taxi in Naples and Colombo, which was the usual practice in those days before organised cruise-style shore excursions were arranged by the ship. They had gazed at the little groups of Arabs sitting around their camp fires by the water's edge as *Canberra* made her first transit of the Suez Canal, and later were thrilled at their first calls in the bustling modern cities of Western and Southern Australia, as they reached their new homeland.

During the voyage, *Canberra* had supplied everything that life could offer. The long days at sea passed with activities which were both pleasurable and profitable, with the educational programmes for the children, the well-stocked library and a superbly equipped cinema for the adults. There were always many children on those voyages, particularly in tourist class. In the dining-room, Margaret Mchugh kept a watchful eye on things at the two children's tables next to her and Mac's places, telling of the unaccompanied little ones who anxiously wanted to try everything on the special children's menu that they should rather have one dish and then a sweet if they finished it.

Helen, who was ten years old and James at the age of eight, were free to explore the ship on their own. Margaret took little Ruth, who was only two, to the playroom up on Games Deck, where they played 'Ring a Ring o' Roses' with the other toddlers and their mothers, while aft, Mac and one of the other Dads from their cabin court kept a fatherly eye on things around the children's swimming pool. Once the children were tucked in for the night, never far from the care of a watchful cabin steward, Mac and Margaret could enjoy the luxury of dancing in the Island Room. They reminded one another that they might never again enjoy the luxury of such a voyage on a great liner.

Ruth turned three on the day *Canberra* arrived in Fremantle, making the day doubly special for the Mchughs. As they left *Canberra* in Sydney they took with them to their new home the charming coloured menu cards and daily programmes as treasured souvenirs which they have kept to this day. Though they have never made such a voyage since, the Mchughs have followed the progress of their very special ship *Canberra* throughout the years. No doubt there are countless others in Australia and New Zealand whose memories are every bit as fond, and who likewise feel that they

*T*he children's play area and pool where Mac Mchugh kept a
fatherly eye on things during the maiden voyage.
The Sun Deck canopy seen in this early
impression was never fitted.

*A* *painting of the 1906 P&O liner* Devanah *from a series of illustrated menu cards, depicting the Line's ships from 1866 to 1937, used on both* Canberra *and* Oriana.

owe the ship some gratitude for helping them start off on the right foot. How many other *Canberra* ephemera have been carefully preserved between the pages of family albums and scrapbooks in places ranging from the homes and flats of Sydney, Melbourne and Auckland to the sheep stations of the Australian outback?

As *Canberra* eventually moved to cruising, her experiences were at first mixed. In New York she had her fair share of those brusque encounters which are a part of everyday life in the 'Big Apple'. After a lightly-patronised and rock-bottom-priced cruise, one passenger told Captain Lefevre, 'I thought your gawd-damn ship was pretty awful'.

Lefevre diffused the man's anger with sympathy, saying, 'I'm sorry you feel that way Sir, My first mate and I spent more than the price of your ticket on dinner in your city last week'. Captain Lefevre had been paid a visit on one of the early New York cruises by a man with a grey fedora cocked at an angle on his head and the butt of a 38-pistol sticking out of his inside jacket pocket. In a flat nasal tone he confronted the master with, 'I hear you got a gamblin' operation goin' on here, we take fifteen per cent off the top – it's for "The Family" you know'. Captain Lefevre offered his uninvited visitor a gin and tonic with the same courtesy which he might have extended to someone such as Lord Kemsley or Sir Donald Bradman, and explained that *Canberra* was a British ship, and that the casino was only opened outside American territorial waters. 'Don't shoot me, go down and see the manager of the Victoria Sporting Club',

Lefevre said, hoping to refer the matter to someone who he thought might be more familiar with that sort of request. This alleged ambassador of 'The Mob' left the ship without incident, while the FBI and British authorities were quietly notified. The man did make a couple of social visits to *Canberra* later, but never pursued any further business.

This was at the beginning of *Canberra's* full-time cruising career when the social role of her crew took on a far greater significance than was ever expected of it in line services. Every cruise passenger expects to meet the ship's captain. Apart from his enormous responsibility for the ship, her navigation, day-to-day operation and, above all, for the safety of everyone aboard, the captain would usually circulate about the decks several times a day. A cruise ship's master is expected to be highly visible socially. While much of the official social activity is shared with the deputy captain, the purser, cruise director and ship's hostesses, it is the captain himself who has his photograph taken with every passenger at receptions during each cruise and every passenger wants to be able to tell his or her friends at home that he had chatted with him socially.

Some of *Canberra's* captains enjoyed the social role more than others. Commodore Wacher tended to be keener on his role as a navigator, whereas Commodores Bradford and Gibb took greater delight in playing host to their passengers. Earlier in her cruising career, when *Canberra* was still one of the largest passenger ships in the world, it was

*T*he social side of the captain's duties during the 1890s as depicted in the venerable *P&O Pencillings*.

customary for Bradford to welcome his passengers at the captain's reception with the words, 'Welcome to *Canberra* – I hope you will find our hospitality to be as big as our ship'. *Canberra's* hospitality has continued to be as big as any newer ship which has since come along.

From the 1970s, captains and other senior officers were allowed to bring their wives along with them, as P&O realised that the presence of the ladies would actually be of benefit to the social roles into which these men found themselves cast. Poor Dorothy Wild was prevented by earlier regulations from joining her husband aboard *Canberra* during his command of the ship through her fitting out and early years of service. She had hoped to sail with him as a passenger aboard the ship after his retirement. Senior officers' children were first permitted aboard on 1 April, 1994. Ian Gibb's wife and two daughters were already waiting for *Canberra* in Piraeus, and actually boarded the ship on 31 March, the day before the change went into effect. While the new policy was indeed no April Fool's Day joke, bungee jumping from the navigating bridge had been rumoured as the day's official gag that year.

All those who have any direct contact with the passengers, be it from the ship's Bureau, behind one of her bars or in the shops, in the dining room, lounges, on deck or in the cabins are in what is today called the hospitality business. Some started from special hotel and cruise ship training institutions and brought with them to *Canberra*

*Hospitality of the bar as seen in this early publicity photograph of the Alice Springs Lounge.*

experience from other ships or from ashore. Others, among them many of the ship's longer serving crew, came up through the ranks in *Canberra*.

Christopher Rodriguez, who rose to the position of assistant supervisor of *Canberra*'s Indian crew, started with P&O during the 1960s. In those days young men were recruited in their home towns in Goa, where in 1498 Vasco de Gama claimed a part of present-day India for his king, bringing Catholicism and the Portuguese language to the Indian subcontinent. They were brought to the ship without passports on a special crew manifest which permitted them direct transfer from the airport to the ship, effectively in customs bond. Once aboard, they learned the job from their experienced older colleagues and the leading hands. They furthered their learning and knowledge with the help of reading materials from the ship's crew library and learned about the world and its peoples as they travelled with the ship. Anyone who was homesick or who had other problems was always

able to seek the help or consolation of someone aboard who came from his own town or village, probably one who also knew his family.

Things changed over the years, with most Indian newcomers having already been professionally trained ashore and also bringing working experience with them. They were recruited in Bombay and travelled to join *Canberra* on their own Indian passports. They formed an enclave of about 400 men within the ship's crew community, being drawn together by a combination of their cultural background, strong family ties and long-standing associations with P&O. A very special part of their religious and social culture travelled with *Canberra* in the form of a Madonna presented to the Goanese crew by a female passenger who was so impressed by their charm, sincerity and faith. It was a statue of Our Lady of the Mystic Rose, from the sixth apparition of the Virgin Mary at Fatima in Portugal on December 7, 1947.

The crew decided to make the statue a circulating centre of prayer and devotion with each of their cabins hosting it for a day. Every evening while *Canberra* was at sea, a small procession would bring the *Rosa Mystica* to the next cabin on the roster, where prayers were said and hymns sung; a small party followed with beer, soft drinks and sandwiches given by the new hosts. The Madonna became known as Mother Mary, and many prayers have been offered through her intervention for such concerns as the recovery of a sick relative far away at home, that a son or daughter should pass school exams, or for the eternal rest of a deceased loved one – and no doubt most often good fortune and plain sailing for *Canberra*, her passengers and company. In thanksgiving for answered prayers, numerous small silver and gold ornaments have been added to the Madonna's robes. These show that 'Mother Mary of the *Canberra*' certainly seems to have kept a very watchful eye on her ship.

The supernatural, in its many manifestations, is generally respected and held in high regard by all ships' crews according to their own beliefs, religious, superstitious or whatever. It probably comes out of a healthy respect for the might of the seas and vulnerability of ships to the hand of Nature. Some of *Canberra*'s crew have long believed that the faces of the characters depicted in the forward stairway murals change to reflect the mood and feeling of the ship.

A prayer printed in the form of a crucifix on the wall above Christopher Rodriguez's desk in the crew office begins with the words, 'The one who reads this prayer shall never drown or burn...' His eyes would scan its closely-set lines as he seated himself to attend to whatever tasks were at hand.

*Canberra*'s Pakistani deck and engine room crews formed a smaller community of some forty or fifty men. Most would be Moslems, with their own place of worship aboard and a similarly close-knit cultural bond among themselves. By the nature of their work, much of it done behind the scenes in the engine room and elsewhere below decks, they were not as much in day-to-day contact with the passengers as their Goanese colleagues from the purser's department. Nonetheless, they were sometimes met carrying out various tasks around the ship and for many years they would sell small wooden ship's life-rings to passengers and visitors to the ship as souvenirs, a traditional privilege which allowed them to raise a little money for charity. On a visit to the bridge one would often see a Pakistani quartermaster on watch at the wheel.

First Engineer David Barraclough, a Yorkshireman who has served aboard *Canberra* since she was commissioned, has spent a good part of his own life aboard. While working on the boilers during *Canberra*'s last refit in November 1996 he pointed out that, 'She is get-

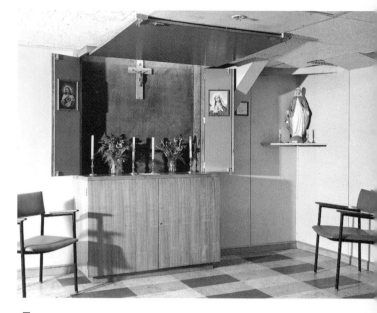

*The altar which serves* Canberra*'s mainly Roman Catholic Goanese and Indian crew.*

ting to be an old lady and now needs rather a lot of taking care of'.

Nonetheless, the turbines still produced the same power as when they were new in 1961, although the ship could no longer make the full 28 knots as her propellers had been changed some years earlier to give maximum performance at the lower speeds used for cruising. The stator coils of her main generators have been rewound, one of them while at sea on a Pacific crossing and the other during a refit in Germany. She has had new evaporators installed, giving her a completely self-sufficient fresh-water distilling capacity of 100 tons per day. The demand for domestic fresh water has increased as cruise passengers take far better care of themselves. Because of the extremely pure water demanded by *Canberra*'s high-performance boilers, passengers and crew are also treated to wonderfully luxuriant baths and showers and incredibly pure drinking water.

*O*ne of Canberra's *Indian quartermasters stands watch at the helm during a cruise.*

One of the most remarkable engineering aspects of *Canberra* has been her enormous electrical power capacity. While many other ships of her vintage have required additional generators to meet the loads demanded by modern cruise services and the passengers themselves, *Canberra's* original machinery continued to supply an abundance of power with capacity to spare. While having to meet the domestic needs of about 2,600 passengers and crew, the added load of ship's services such as air conditioning, laundry and sewage disposal add up to a capacity that ashore would suffice for a town of some 10,000 inhabitants. A sewage treatment plant was installed in 1979, and a complete waste management system subsequently implemented, keeping *Canberra* up to date with the latest international environmental protection standards.

Many of those who work behind the scenes have been brought into contact with passengers who have had special needs of one sort or another. This could be for something as simple as retrieving a piece of jewellery or someone's dentures from the ship's plumbing, to meeting special medical or dietary needs. *Canberra's* chief baker, John Herbert, was asked on one cruise to make a special soda bread for a passenger on a very specific diet. The passenger was so delighted with the bread that he insisted on having John's recipe for later use at home. The same person later returned to *Canberra* for another cruise when, as it happened, a relief baker was aboard. The bread was not quite up to Herbert's standard and, while not dissatisfied, the passenger wrote a letter to P&O Cruises explaining that he wanted to be sure that in future his cruises would coincide with the chief

baker's schedule so that he could enjoy the same delicious bread aboard *Canberra*!

Another cruise passenger, Jack Jacobs, wanted John to make a particular dessert called 'stuffed monkeys'. After some persuasion and being given a recipe the baker acquiesced, and the confection was offered as a dessert choice on the dinner menu one evening as 'Jack Jacobs's stuffed monkeys'. Jacobs was so delighted that he collected as many spare copies of the menu as he could get his hands on. He asked John to autograph one of them as a souvenir and no doubt distributed the others to his friends and family at home.

The bar stewards were among those who always had the greatest amount of day-to-day contact with passengers, particularly at the sit-up bars. John Gedge was himself something of an institution in the Cricketer's, with his vast knowledge of the game, its history, statistics and up-to-the-minute results and team standings. Peter Steele,

*Much of what goes on behind the scenes in a cruise ship such as* Canberra *has to do with feeding the passengers and crew. Even the bread and pastries are freshly baked on board every day.*

who had tried to do the Argentine prisoner's trick of squeezing over the top of the Century Bar doors, has made many friends over a number of years among those he served in that spot's intimate interior. He recalls one of his 'regulars' who at other times of the day would occupy one particular chair in the Promenade deck lobby outside the Meridian Lounge for hours on end. If he found his chair occupied, he would sit opposite it and glare at its occupant until he or she moved. He became known as Jack the Chair. Peter suggested that whenever *Canberra* ended her days, 'P&O should send that chair to Jack as a souvenir of all the hours he has spent in it'.

A man from Andorra boarded for the world cruise one year, and took a letter from his physician round to all the bartenders. It instructed that he was not to be served any alcohol, and he asked for their support in keeping him 'on the wagon' throughout the voyage. Peter recalled that as the man dried out, he would occasionally get a bit 'ratty' with the bar staff, but they kept him off the bottle as they had promised him they would. He ended up staying aboard *Canberra* for the entire summer season. The ship's company were no

*Any romances that flourish on board have to compete with the romance of the ship herself as she steams silently among the places which passengers and crew alike dream of.*

doubt glad enough to see him finally leave, as he had started to get bored and to find fault with things, nitpick and complain.

Not everyone has Audrey McGaw's capacity to thrive on shipboard life over such long periods of time. Indeed some passengers on the world

cruises would start getting bored and irritable after only a month or so.

On a cruise in the 1970s, everyone in the Bonito Club, including *Canberra*'s master, were given a bit of a surprise one evening. A tall statuesque lady entered the room alone, wearing a fur coat and high stiletto-heeled shoes. She walked right across the dance floor to the edge of the pool without speaking a word to anyone. There she shed the coat over a nearby chair, kicked off the high heels and jumped stark naked into the pool. Everyone's eyes were firmly rooted to the young woman as an officer fished her out of the water, covering her with his own jacket. At the same time a chorus of high-pitched wifely voices chanted at their husbands such things as, 'Albert; don't you dare look'. Too late!

The purser's office and ship's hostesses have always been an oasis of help and comfort to passengers in all sorts of situations. These ran from settling differences between incompatible shipmates in shared cabins to helping people with shore excursion arrangements, exchanging currency and offering various pieces of personal advice. They provided support in special cases and were in effect the caring heart of the ship. One passenger, for instance, who had saved up for a long time for a cruise which would enable him to return to a bar he had frequented in Gibraltar during the war, was devastated to find when he got there that the place had closed down years earlier. When he returned to *Canberra*, he confided his bitter disappointment to one of the ship's hostesses, who kept a friendly eye on him over the rest of the cruise. As long-serving deputy purser James Cusick, said, 'A ship without people is a ship without a heart'.

It is the passengers themselves more than any other influence which make a ship as popular and well-loved as *Canberra*. They, after all, buy the cruises and book the voyages, and it is their comfort, wellbeing and safety which the ship's crew have to provide for and for which the ship was designed and built in the first place. A ship such as *Canberra* has to be capable of catering for all eventualities of life from the cradle to the grave. Of all that can go on during a voyage or cruise, it is romance which is the most celebrated aspect of passengers' lives at sea. Over her long life, *Canberra* indeed has had her share of romantic tales.

Although ships' captains are not permitted to perform marriages, there have been a number of weddings arranged along the way during *Canberra*'s cruises, and particularly on the world voyages. There was, for instance, one couple who met at the beginning of a world cruise, fell in love, and made arrangements to be married ashore in Hong Kong during the voyage, returning home to England as husband and wife at the end of what was also to be a glorious honeymoon. In cases such as these, the couple would return to the ship after their wedding ceremony ashore for a blessing given by a chaplain in *Canberra*'s elegant Crystal Room, followed by a reception with their shipmates. Sadly, on one such occasion the groom had the misfortune to die on board only two weeks after the marriage, landing his poor bride back home as a widow.

*Canberra* has also been somewhat of a marriage market for her crew. People were drawn to the ship's cloistered crew environment which took them to exotic and romantic places which they dream about all their lives. Suffice it to say that most marriage opportunities were to be found in the purser's departments, although a number of engineers and officers have found brides aboard the ship too.

There was one premeditated instance of a widower who planned a shipboard affair with a lady who would do the world cruise with him on the

*Tugs hold* Canberra*'s stern in check while manoeuvring in Vancouver early in her career, three quarters of a world away from her home port in Southampton.*

took you so long?' He then realised that she had been waiting for him. They were soon together again and talking about returning to *Canberra* as soon as they could.

Not all shipboard romances were, however, entirely above board. A lady came to the bridge one evening and told the officer on watch that she thought her husband had jumped overboard, explaining that the man was prone to being depressive and suggesting that he might have attempted suicide. The officer thought that there might be something more to the story, and questioned the lady as to where and when she had last seen her husband. A discreet behind-the-scenes telephone call to the Peacock Room bartender confirmed that the man had indeed been there about an hour earlier and also revealed that he had been seen leaving the room with a tall blonde woman on his arm. Once her identity and cabin number were established, the night purser, Susan Jones, and an officer were sent below to the lady's room. The woman called out from behind the room's locked door that she was quite alone, but Susan's womanly intuition in such matters told her otherwise. Brandishing her pass-key she quickly unlocked the door and asked the sur-

understanding that once the voyage was over they would go their separate ways without keeping in touch with each other. The trip was a great success and the couple enjoyed themselves thoroughly. They said goodbye in Southampton and went their separate ways. However, the man, who shared a house with his grown-up daughter, moped so much afterwards that she felt something must be wrong. He had apparently not told her anything about his cruise partner. Finally, she got the story out of him, and realised why he was feeling so blue. She suggested that there would be no harm in at least telephoning the lady, but he insisted that he had to keep his side of the bargain. Finally, in exasperation, the daughter told him that if he would not call the lady, she would find her number and do so herself on his behalf. When he eventually did make the call and the lady asked him, 'what

prised occupant, 'if you are alone, then who belongs to those feet sticking out from under the curtains?' The hapless Romeo was seen later sitting in a lounge chair with his head in his hands, muttering sorrowfully to himself.

For many, cruising is more a celebration of the romance of life itself in pleasant surroundings and good company while travelling to distant ports. Alice Lovely was, so to speak, a charter member of *Canberra*'s worldwide 'family' of loyal passengers. After making the maiden voyage, she has returned to the ship often, and, at the time of writing, was booked on the final cruise from Southampton on 10 September 1996 at the age of ninety-four years. *Canberra* had taken on a very special significance, particularly since the untimely death of her only daughter some years earlier. No longer having family of her own, apart from her grandchildren, the ship, her officers and crew, and the many people Alice knows and meets regularly during her many voyages and cruises, have become her new adopted worldwide family.

Alice usually travelled with a woman friend in inner court cabins C9 or C11, up forward below the Meridian Lounge. She preferred the larger tables for six or

eight people in the Pacific Restaurant, seldom having the same table partners from one cruise to another. One of her favourite spots has always been the Crow's Nest with its panoramic forward outlook over *Canberra*'s bow.

Neither a drinker nor a gambler, Alice nonetheless has always been at the centre of her circles of friends aboard *Canberra*. One evening her friends introduced her to the horse racing game. They told her that they were all betting on a particular horse, and that she really should 'get in too'. She placed a modest bet, and then found out that she had been named as the jockey. This, she found out, meant that she had to turn the handle which moved the wooden horse along its track. As she started to crank the handle she was at first dismayed that her 'mount' didn't appear to be moving. Once assured by a nearby ship's officer that she was doing just

*Star Princess will become Canberra's successor, reviving the name Arcadia.*

fine, she cranked the horse to a decisive victory, not realising that she had won as her attention had been resolutely focused on turning the handle without looking at the horse at all. But that was only the run-off, and she went on to win the final race. All her friends started putting their winnings into the cup she was holding, insisting that she should keep the money. Instead she gave the winnings to the sponsoring seamen's charity.

Early in another cruise she had been talking to the ship's dance instructor, and mentioned that she would love to have a dance with someone who could really waltz. He promised her a dance, but, as the days passed, she began to wonder if perhaps he had forgotten. As the orchestra struck up their very last number for the cruise, the instructor took the microphone and announced that he would have the last dance with a very special lady, and called Alice Lovely to the dance floor. As he expertly led her in an English waltz under the spotlights, she mentioned to him that there seemed to be so much room to dance without anyone else getting in the way. 'That's because they're all watching us', he told her.

*Canberra*'s distinguished career has touched the lives of millions, from the Belfast shipbuilders to the veterans of the D-Day landings. To those who have worked on *Canberra* though the years such as John Herbert, David Barraclough, Mike Bradford and Rory Smith, who was the last captain of *Canberra* and will be the first master of *Arcadia*, and to those who joined her in the beginning, her retirement will be a sad moment in their professional lives. To Alice Lovely, who was one of *Canberra*'s first passengers and who will be among the last, and those such as Sir Hugh Casson, whose involvement has made the ship dear to their hearts and who have been regular visitors throughout her career, *Canberra* will be greatly missed. Dame Pattie Menzies, sponsor of the great ship, last visited her in 1992 and sadly passed away in the summer of 1995.

Perhaps one of the most poignant thoughts to be expressed about *Canberra* as her illustrious career draws to a close, was a comment made by one of her long-serving crew who said, 'There has always been a *Canberra*'. Indeed, with a solid thirty-five years of service to her credit, encompassing working as a troop ship and being part of the D-Day anniversary flotilla alongside her regular career, *Canberra* has shown that she is, most certainly, a legend of a ship.

*Dame Pattie Menzies on board* Canberra *with her grandaughter and Captain Ian Gibb in 1991.*

*Long after she is gone and her name is taken from Lloyd's Register of Ships,* Canberra *will continue to sail on in the hearts and minds of the thousands who have travelled aboard her and served in her.*

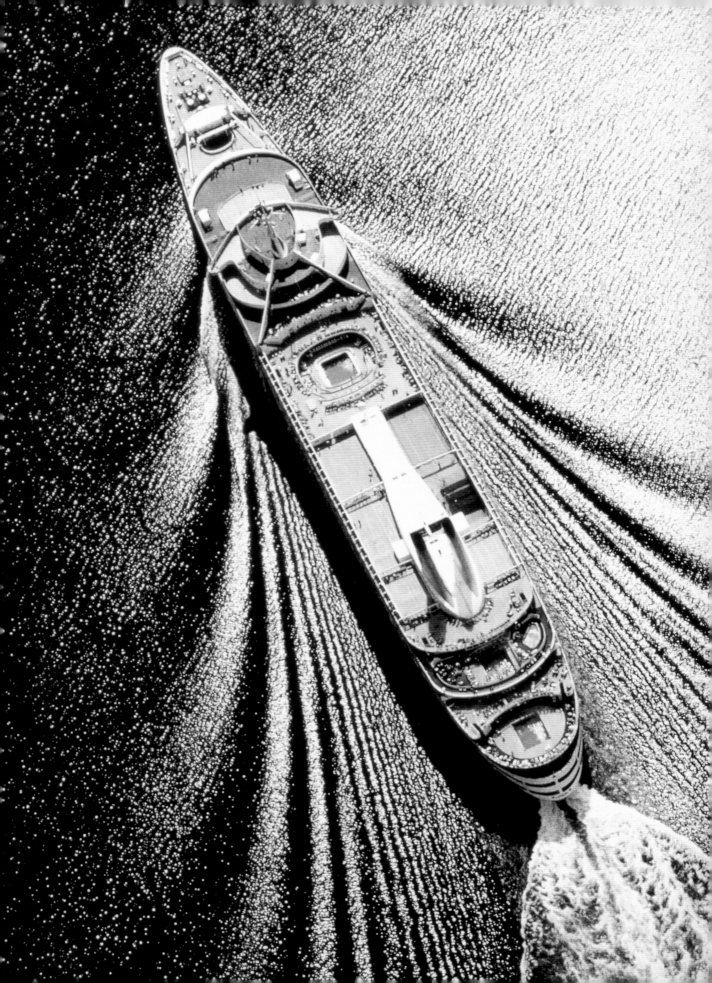

# EPILOGUE

## CANBERRA: THE ABORIGINAL WORD
## FOR 'MEETING PLACE'

During the thirty-six years that this great lady has sailed the oceans of the world, nearly one million passengers have enjoyed and appreciated her warmth, intimacy, grace and strength, meeting others from all walks of life. She has, sometimes almost alone, provided the British public with their own special brand of cruising and she will long be fondly remembered by thousands of people to whom cruising became a way of holiday life.

In her early years she and her first cousin, *Oriana*, dominated the last great period of liner voyages to Australia. Though the special character of that period may appear dim in the memories of most of us, she nevertheless forged great ties of affection with the thousands of Australians who travelled in her and who have fond memories of this unique ship.

The list of Captains that have commanded *Canberra* is long and includes great maritime names of the recent past. As the final name on that list one wonders how such an honour came my way. Nevertheless, it is indeed a great honour to have commanded *Canberra*, without doubt one of the finest great ships to have flown the red ensign. She had already made her name when I joined my first P&O ship in London. Little did I know that one day I would actually command the fabled lady. She has always been part of P&O throughout my entire career to date, and though in September she will have her last, and arguably her finest, hour under the famous house flag of P&O, she will always retain a special corner of my affections. Mine, and the thousands of those who have sailed with her over the years.

She is much loved and she will be long remembered.

Captain Rory Smith
Master, SS *Canberra*

*Celebrations of a cruising legend; streamers over* Canberra *at sunset.*

## LIST OF CAPTAINS

*An original watercolour by Canberra's architect Sir Hugh Casson depicting P&O's most famous cruise liner off Cowes early in her career.*

## PICTURE ACKNOWLEDGEMENTS

Illustrations are from the P&O archives and P&O publications, except those which are reproduced by courtesy of the following: the Ulster Folk and Transport Museum pp17, 42; Denis Griffiths pp23, 142; the author pp31, 33 (l&r), 50-1, 92-3, 129, 158; the collection of Mike Bradford pp49, 73, 100, 130; the collection of Jim Davis pp58-9, 64-6, 75; the collection of Rosemary Sinclair (neé Fenton) p67; the collection of Jim Hale p91; Mrs K M Lane p104 (below); M&Y Photo Agency, Portsmouth p106; the Imperial War Museum pp111, 114; Paul Hayley, *Soldier* Magazine p115; Russel S Ireland p116; *The News*, Portsmouth p133; Fairfax photo library, Australia p164.

Cartoons are from the P&O archives, and are reproduced with grateful thanks to the *Daily Mail* p84; Express Newspapers Plc p87; the Solo Agency and, Mac p132, top; and Jak p132, bottom.

The following artists have been kind enough to give their permission for reproduction of their work: Sir Hugh Casson ppiii, 168; Ronald Dean, by courtesy of BAIN HOGG GROUP p112; Jim Petrie, by courtesy of ARL Editions p134; Tim Thompson p150-1.

*R.M.S. Canberra — off Cowes.*